The Furniture Factory Outlet Guide

2016 Edition

by

Kimberly Causey

Published by:

Home Decor Press
P. O. Box 671312
Marietta, GA 30066

To order paperback copies of this book, or any other books published by Home Decor Press, please visit our website at www.smartdecorating.com Our titles are also available through Ingram Book Co.

If you have any questions or comments regarding this book, please write to the author in care of the publisher at the above address.

Publisher's Cataloging-in-Publication Data

Causey, Kimberly,

The Furniture Factory Outlet Guide, 2016 Edition
Includes index.

      1. Interior decoration--United States
      2. Consumer education--United States
      3. Shopping--United States

ISBN13 978-1-888229-49-3
ISBN 1-888229-49-7

This book is designed to provide information about the home furnishings industry based upon the personal experience and research of the author. The information and recommendations given in this book strictly reflect only the author's opinions and personal knowledge of the products, services, people, companies, and all other topics discussed herein.

The author's sole purpose in writing this book is to present information and consumer advice that may benefit readers. The author and publisher do not intend to provide legal, accounting, or medical advice. If expert assistance is required, please consult a qualified professional.

Table of Contents

Table of Contents

Factory Outlets and Discounters

Table of Contents

Factory Outlets and Discounters

Frequently Asked Questions

How much money can I save if I buy my furniture from the sources listed in this book?

You will save 40% to 50% if you buy new, first-quality furniture in any style or color over the phone or via a web site.

You will save 50% to 80% if you travel to the factory outlets in person and buy new, first-quality furniture.

You will save 80% to 90% if you travel to the factory outlets in person and buy furniture that requires minor repairs or touchups.

Are all furniture brands available at these savings?

The vast majority of brands are available at these savings: Henredon, Maitland-Smith, Marge Carson, Vanguard, Hickory White, Century, Broyhill, La-Z-Boy, Kincaid, and thousands more.

A few manufacturers have chosen to restrict their furniture from being sold by factory outlets and deep discounters, notably Thomasville and Drexel-Heritage.

Fortunately, competition among manufacturers helps consumers get around restrictive pricing. For every piece of furniture from a manufacturer with high restricted minimum pricing, there are dozens of competing manufacturers making furniture that is substantially identical in looks and quality at a lower price.

Why do prices often vary so widely on the identical pieces of furniture?

Good question. It all depends on where you shop.

Here's a great example. The chair on the left and the chair on the right were made

    ...in the same factory
    ...by the same workers
    ...according to the same standards of quality
    ...from the same inventories of wood, springs, and leather.

In terms of quality and design, there is absolutely no difference between these two chairs.

So, why does the chair on the left cost $1,699.00 when the chair on the right costs only $999.00?

The one and only difference between these two chairs is the *location in which they are being sold.*

The $1,699.00 "Manhattan" chair in the photo on the left was photographed in a local retail Pottery Barn store in a high rent shopping center.

The $999.00 "Manhattan" chair in the photo on the right was photographed in the Mitchell Gold + Bob Williams factory outlet in Hickory, NC. Mitchell Gold + Bob Williams manufactures the entire line of Pottery Barn upholstered furniture in their factory in Taylorsville, NC. It wasn't damaged or defective in any way.

So, why would you pay $700.00 more to buy the chair on the left?

When you buy from a local furniture retailer, the final price you pay usually depends on how much money the retailer spends on advertising, expensive retail stores in high-rent areas, and beautiful catalogs sent out free in the mail. All of those things cost a lot of money, and all of those costs are recouped from the average consumer who accepts high prices.

Smart furniture shoppers make sure all they pay for is beautiful high-quality furniture. The best way to do that is to buy directly from the manufacturer, skipping all the middleman markups added by local furniture retailers.

How can I find the lowest price available on a particular piece of furniture?

Check my website: **www.smartdecorating.com**.

I use my manufacturing contacts to find the lowest prices available to the general public, and post them on my website.

You can aso use the "Ask Kimberly" feature to get quick answers on furniture bargains!

Are there certain times of the year when I can get extra discounts?

Yes! Many factory outlets and deep discounters have special "after market" sales in May and November. These sales happen shortly after the semi-annual wholesale furniture markets in High Point, NC.

When the wholesale markets end, many manufacturers send all their floor samples to the factory outlets, and most outlets have special sales to move out all the extra furniture. Discounts frequently run 75% to 80% off retail during these times.

Some factory outlets have sales right before the High Point market. Typically, you'll save an extra 10%-20% off the already discounted outlet price of 50%-80% off retail.

Some factory outlets also have sales in January and July when business is slow. No matter what time of year you're shopping for furniture, there will be some very good sales coming up within the next month or two.

Please check my web site, www.smartdecorating.com, for free information about upcoming sales at factory outlets and furniture factories.

What should I bring with me to a factory outlet?

1. Simple sketches of each room you intend to decorate, with the basic room dimensions shown. Snapshots of each room are very useful, as well.

2. Measurements of all doorways and hallways that your furniture will have to go through to reach the correct room.

   Take special care to measure any turns or landings in your stairway. Sometimes, large pieces of furniture get stuck on stairways because they can't round the corner.

3. Swatches of any fabrics, carpeting, or paint that you'll need when choosing upholstered furniture.

4. Pictures of basic styles you like (and those you hate). This can be a very useful way to narrow down the look you want (and the looks you want to avoid).

5. Tape measure to measure any furniture you are considering buying. Outlets generally don't have any to lend.

How will my furniture be shipped to me?

Most factory outlets and deep discounters use "white glove" furniture delivery services that will unpack your furniture and set it up in the correct place in your home, including carrying it up or down stairs if needed.

Furniture delivery people will generally not provide the following services: moving your old furniture, taking away packing materials, and putting electronic equipment into entertainment centers.

How long will it take to receive my furniture?

If you're shopping in person at the factory outlet or deep discounter and you find the furniture you want in stock, you can normally have your furniture shipped to you immediately. This is another big advantage to going to North Carolina in person. Not only do you get substantially better discounts, there's no wait for your furniture. Typical delivery will run 1-2 weeks, depending on how far away from North Carolina you live.

If you special order your furniture from a deep discounter, you will normally have to wait 8-12 weeks for your furniture to be delivered. Just like local furniture retailers, furniture deep discounters custom-order your furniture directly from the manufacturer.

How much will the freight charges be to have my furniture shipped home?

The freight charges will depend on the weight of the furniture. The factory outlet or deep discounter will be able to give you a written quote at the time you place your order or buy your furniture in person.

Most types of furniture will cost about 5% of the retail price to ship to the continental United States using a "white glove delivery" carrier. "White glove delivery" typically includes having your furniture unpacked, placed in the correct room, and assembled if necessary.

A few companies offer free delivery, particularly on upholstery. Free delivery usually includes delivery only to your doorstep or just inside your home. Customers who wish to have the furniture unpacked, assembled, or moved to the correct room will usually need to pay an upcharge.

One way to save on freight costs is to purchase your furniture at a furniture factory outlet mall that offers combined shipping for all of your purchases from different showrooms. By far, the biggest shipping savings come from having your furniture shipped all at one time via the same carrier.

The Hickory Furniture Mart in Hickory, NC, has the widest variety of furniture at factory outlet prices that can be combined in the same shipment to save on shipping costs.

If I order my furniture over the phone, do I have to pay sales tax on it?

If you order your furniture over the phone from outside of North Carolina and have it delivered directly to your home in another state, you will not have to pay any North Carolina sales tax.

Whether or not you will have to pay sales tax to your own home state depends on the laws where you live. At this writing, most states have laws requiring consumers to pay "use tax" on any items purchased from an out of state vendor if no sales tax was paid at the time of purchase.

States are becoming more aggressive recently in enforcing existing use tax laws. Many states inspect trucks bringing furniture into the state and assess use tax and penalties against the purchaser if sales tax has not been paid, including California, Florida, and Texas..

In an effort to do the right thing by their customers, some North Carolina furniture discounters do charge sales tax and submit it to the state to which your furniture is delivered.

Some smaller furniture discounters don't charge sales tax on out of state deliveries, leaving it to the buyer to take care of any sales tax owed. They aren't necessarily doing the customer any favors. I've heard from a lot of angry consumers over the years who received surprise tax bills from their home states months after their furniture arrived.

The best course of action for any consumer is to contact the sales tax office in your own state and find out if use tax is owed on purchases from out of state. If you do owe use tax in your state on your furniture purchase, the best thing to do is to simply pay it at the time of purchase.

Can I buy custom draperies, fabrics, wallcoverings, carpeting, rugs, blinds, accessories, and other furnishings at a discount, too?

Absolutely. All of these things can be purchased directly from manufacturers, deep discounters, factory outlets, and local wholesale workrooms. For more information, please read chapters 3 through 18 of my book, _The Insider's Guide To Buying Home Furnishings_.

Can I use a professional interior designer and still get my furniture at a discount?

Certainly. I've found that some consumers believe that they must make a trade-off between price and service. They think that if they choose to buy their furniture from a factory outlet or deep discounter which doesn't provide an in-home design service, they can't have any in-home design help. This isn't at all the case.

There are many interior designers who work on an hourly basis. It is a simple matter to hire a designer at an hourly rate for her design advice only, and then go buy your furniture directly from the factory outlets and deep discounters. In this way, you still get the best possible price, and you can get the service you need.

Another advantage to hiring a designer this way is that you only pay for the help you actually need and no more. If you buy your furniture through a local retailer and use their "free" in-home design help, what you're actually doing is paying a large mark-up on everything you buy to compensate the designer for his or her time.

Everyone pays the same mark-up whether they need to consult with the designer for an hour, a week, or a month. So, customers who only need a little help choosing their colors and arranging their furniture pay the same hefty commission as those customers who need far more assistance. This is hardly a fair system.

You can't go wrong hiring a designer by the hour. This way, you only pay for exactly the help you actually need and receive.

For detailed information on locating a reputable and qualified designer in your area, negotiating a fair hourly rate, putting together a contract, and making sure the job is done properly, please read chapter 14 of my book, _The Insider's Guide To Buying Home Furnishings_ .

What do I do if there's a problem with my order?

Statistically, you are far less likely to have a problem with a factory outlet or deep discounter than you are with your local furniture dealer. Just ask anyone who put down a deposit for furniture at Sears Homelife, Heilig-Meyers, Krause's, Castro Convertibles, or any of the hundreds of other furniture retailers who have gone bankrupt in the last few years. Still, every year a few problems do occur with furniture ordered from North Carolina.

As you'll see in the detailed reviews in this book, I do take special care to investigate and track each store's reputation for customer service over time. If at all possible, stick with the sources that have no negative marks on their customer service record.

The best defense is prevention. As you'll read in the individual outlet reviews, the sources with the best bargains tend to also be the most reputable.

What if the furniture brand I want is only available "to the trade"?

Go shop at the "to the trade" showroom. Anyone can, and many do.

For many years, my family's factory had showrooms at the world trade centers in Atlanta and Dallas, and we also showed at the International Home Furnishings Market in High Point, NC. During all the years I worked in those showrooms, I watched many consumers come in and shop for themselves. Some were friends and relatives of furniture store owners and others in the trade, but many had simply figured out how to get in on their own.

The Los Angeles Times interviewed Elaine M. Redfield, president of the American Society Of Interior Designers (ASID) for the Los Angeles area, about consumers getting into design centers and wholesale showrooms to buy directly from manufacturers. Ms. Redfield had this to say: "It's a simple matter for someone to get a resale number and go shop at the showrooms, and many do."

The Los Angeles Times also interviewed Pat Stamps, the former head of the ASID for the Los Angeles area. She had this to say about retail customers getting into the wholesale showrooms to shop: "We all know it happens because our customers tell us they've shopped here. I've seen women who come in who use their husband's resale number, and he sells plants."

In my experience, about 3/4 of the manufacturers out there will sell directly to consumers at their wholesale showrooms. Of course, it is important to know how to get into the showrooms and how to properly conduct business once you get there.

Wholesale shopping is not at all like shopping at a local retail store. You must have tact, discretion, and a good working knowledge of how business is conducted between interior decorators and wholesale sources. It's also important to have the proper credentials, including a resale number.

For more detailed information on how to get into wholesale showrooms and design centers, and how to shop properly once you get there, please read chapter 19 of my book, _The Insider's Guide To Buying Home Furnishings_ .

How can I make sure I'm buying high-quality furniture?

This is too broad a subject to go into here. For detailed information on furniture construction, wood types, and fabric types, please see my website, **www.smartdecorating.com**.

How can I obtain updated information on the outlets and deep discounters in this book?

Visit my web site, **www.smartdecorating.com**, to receive updated information on the deep discounters and factory outlets reviewed in this book. You may also wish to follow me on Twitter at @KimberlyCausey to receive urgent news of special sales, discounts, and consumer warnings. I also post furniture bargain news on my Facebook page.

I always let my readers know which stores may have moved, closed, or received customer service complaints since the last book printing. I also let my readers know about new sources I've found, special sales coming up, bargains on hotel rooms, etc.

What do the star ratings in this book mean?

★★★★★   Extreme discounts and unique inventory. Don't miss!

★★★★   Above average. Well worth a visit.

★★★   Average.

★★   Disappointing prices and selection.

★   Avoid.

Factory Outlets and Discounters

Adams Furniture

★★

301 North Main St, High Point, NC, 27262

Hours: Monday-Friday 9:30-5:30,
Saturday 10:00-5:00
Phone: 336-889-0807
Email: adamsfurniture@triad.rr.com
Website: adamsfurniture.com
Discount: Wholesale pricing to public
Payment: VISA, MasterCard, Personal
Check
Delivery: Store uses outside shippers

The Adams Furniture Factory Outlet has undergone a recent, dramatic change. They no longer carry the beautiful high-end English reproduction furniture that made them such a great shopping destination for so many years. I'm sorry to lose what was once such a unique source of gorgeous case goods.

Now the outlet is filled with plain upholstered furniture, most of which are in some shade of beige. All of the samples here available for retail sale appear to be the basic beige samples for Adams Furniture's custom lines available to decorators only.

The prices and quality are fine, but there's little in the way of beauty or originality here. No wonder they have big signs banning all photography inside the showroom. As you can see from the photo I was able to take through the front window, the furniture here is very plain and unremarkable.

Inside, I saw a plain beige linen sofa for $1,495.00 and a matching armchair for $595.00, neither of which is much of a bargain.

You can find much better style for less money at other more convenient locations in North Carolina and Virginia. In particular, I would suggest the factory outlets for Broyhill, La-Z-Boy, Kincaid, Vanguard, Hooker, Hickory White, Century, and Henredon.

You can do so much better. Please see the other listings in this book for upholstery sources with much more variety to offer.

Alan Ferguson Associates ★★

1212 N. Main St., High Point, NC, 27262

Hours: Monday-Friday 9:00-5:00, Saturday 10:00-4:00
Phone: 336-889-3866
Email: sales@alanferguson.com
Website: None
Discount: 40%-50% off mfr retail
Payment: VISA, MasterCard, Personal Check
Delivery: White glove delivery

Alan Ferguson has moved to a new location in High Point, a few blocks away from their long time location next to now defunct Atrium Furniture Mall. They carry a mix of new furniture and antiques.

I find their new showroom to be much more traditional, lacking the fun contemporary flair of the old store. Shoppers looking for the kind of unique contemporary lighting, furniture, and accessories that were available at the old location for Alan Ferguson Associates might want to check out Reflections Contemporary Furnishings at the Hickory Furniture Mart.

Alan Ferguson Associates have also changed their focus away from discounting furniture nationwide. They promote themselves primarily as a local interior design service, not a national discounter. Visitors to the area specifically looking for a wide variety of deeply discounted furniture will find their time better spent elsewhere.

They are certainly a very honest company. Alan Ferguson Associates is one of the oldest furniture dealers in High Point. They have a spotless record with the BBB, and I've never had a single reader complaint about them.

Overall, Alan Ferguson Associates is not in a convenient location for out of town shoppers, and it has little to offer in the way of extraordinary style or value that would justify taking the time to drive to old downtown High Point. I would recommend instead that shoppers visit more conveniently located stores in North Carolina and Virginia that offer better deals, such as Hickory Park, the Henredon Factory Outlet, or Boulevard Bazaar.

Vendor carries 66 manufacturer's lines

American Leather
Ann Gish
Ardley Hall
Arte de Mexico
Arteriors
Artisan House, inc
Artistic Frame
Bauer International
Bolier
Brown Jordan
Brunschwig & Fils
C. R. Currin
Cambridge Carpets
Camelot Carpet Mills
Camilla House Imports
Currey & Co.
Distinctive Carpet
Duralee Fabrics
Emerson et Cie
Fabricut
FFDM
Fine Art Lamps

G. C. Craftsmen
George Kovacs Lighting
Global Views, Inc.
Gloster
Jamie Young Lamps
John-Richard
Johnston Casuals
Kingsley-Bate
KNF Designs
Kravet Fabrics
La Barge
Lake Shore Studios
Lee Industries
Lloyd/Flanders
Lorts
Luna Bella
Maitland-Smith
Mariposa
Masland Carpet & Rugs
Mathews and Company
Morgan Hill
Murray Feiss Lighting

Napa Home and Garden
Old Biscayne Designs
Osborne & Little
Pindler & Pindler
Quoizel
Robert Allen Fabrics
Robertex Associates
S. Harris & Co.
Sarreid
Scalamandre Fabrics
Schumacher Fabrics
Sonneman
Speer Collectables
Stark Carpets
Stonegate Designs
Swaim
Thayer Coggin
Theodore Alexander
Trowbridge Gallery
Visual Comfort
Whitecraft Rattan
Younger

14

American Accents

★★★★

Furniture Avenue Galleries - 4350 Furniture Ave., Jamestown, NC, 27282

Hours: Monday-Saturday 9:30-6:00
Phone: 336-885-1304
Email: info@americanaccentsfurniture.com
Website: americanaccentsfurniture.com
Discount: 35%-40% off mfr retail
Payment: Personal Check
Delivery: White glove delivery

American Accents has had an excellent reputation for quality and service for many years. They specialize in high-quality shaker and early American reproductions. They sell American-made solid wood furniture (case goods) only, no imports. You will find a few upholstered pieces around the showroom at great prices, but this is not their focus.

This store has excellent service and a spotless record with the BBB. I've never heard a single reader complaint about them. I've been very pleased with the service my own design clients have received here.

They have some great deals on high quality furniture from companies like Simply Amish, Penns Creek, Brown Street, and more. Simply Amish has some very nice modern designs.

On a recent visit, I found a great deal on a solid maple dining room set from Simply Amish in new, first quality condition (pictured on the next page). This set retails for $17,942.00, but you could get this nine piece set for only $7,999.00, a savings of over 55% off retail!

All of the furniture here is very well constructed of solid oak, maple, and cherry. It's a bit more expensive than the cheap imports, but it will look great for many years. If you like a contemporary or transitional look, but you want the quality of an American made product, American Accents is a great place to shop!

Bargain tip: Don't miss the after market sales!

Simply Amish dining room set at American Accents

Retail: $17,942.00 Discounted price: $7,999.00
Savings at American Accents: $9,943.00 = 55% off retail

Vendor carries 35 manufacturer's lines

Bassett

Big Sky Carvers

Bradco Chair Co.

Brown Street

Cape Craftsmen

Carolina's Choice

Cassady

Cast Classics

Charleston Forge

Cherry Pond

Classic Rattan

Conover Chair

E. R. Buck

Edrich Mills Wood Shop

Friendship Upholstery

Heritage House

Kingsley-Bate

Lt. Moses Willard

Masterfield

McKay Table Pads

Mobel

Mohawk

Null Furniture

Ohio Table Pad

Orderest Bedding

P & P Chair

Park Place

Penns Creek

Philadelphia

Phillips Furniture

Simply Amish

Skillcraft

The Ashton Company

The Chair Co.

Two Day Designs

Amish Oak and Cherry

★★★★★

Hickory Furniture Mart - U. S. Hwy 70 SE, Level 2, Hickory, NC, 28602

Hours: Monday-Saturday 9:00-6:00
Phone: 828-261-4776
Email: sales@amishoakandcherry.com
Website: amishoakandcherry.com
Discount: 50% to 60% off mfr retail
Payment: VISA, MasterCard, Discover, Personal Check
Delivery: White glove delivery

Amish Oak and Cherry is a great source for genuine Amish furniture in North Carolina. Their quality is top notch. Each piece is solid oak or solid cherry. They also use a 15 step catalyzed finish on each piece that makes it highly resistant to scratches, spills, and other damage. The finish looks great as well.

They also carry a variety of outside lines, including Oakwood Interiors, Keystone Collections, and MacKenzie Dow. If you are interested in a more urban look, Keystone Collections offers several contemporary/transitional collections that will have the look of popular national brands, but at much better quality.

On a recent visit, I found a great deal here on a solid maple bedroom set in a very attractive contemporary style, pictured on the following page. The queen sleigh bed, dresser, chest, and two nightstands retail for $12,565.00, but you could buy this set in new first quality condition for only $6,885.00, which is a savings of $5,680.00 or 45% off retail. Plus, during the after market sale, you could save an extra 10%, bringing the price down to $6,197.00, 51% off retail.

You'll find a wide variety of furniture styles here: Shaker, Mission, contemporary, transitional, and traditional. They now offer leather furniture from Leathercraft and Distinction Leather, as well as upholstery from Jetton. You'll also find a nice selection of children's furniture here.

Amish Oak and Cherry has always given excellent service to my design clients, and I've never heard a single reader complaint about them. They are by far the best source in the Hickory, NC area for Amish furniture.

Solid maple bedroom set at Amish Oak & Cherry

Retail: $12,565.00 Discounted price: $6,197.00
Savings at Amish Oak & Cherry: $6,368.00 = 51% off retail

Vendor carries 128 manufacturer's lines

Abner Henry	Black Mountain	Delafield
Amish Oak and Cherry	Bordeaux	Dutch Creek
Amish Oak Cabin	Bridge Bay	Elegant River Bend
Amish Oak Nursery	Bridgewood Dining	Elizabeth Lockwood
Amish Oak Office	Brunswick	Empire Bedroom
Arcadia Furniture	Bryson Bedroom	Empress
Arts and Crafts Ind.	Burlington	Englander Bedding
Arvada Dining	Canal Dover	English Shaker
Ashton Picture Co.	Canterbury	Estate
Aspen Furniture	Carter Furniture	Fur Elise
Aspen Valley	Chateau	Georgetown
Avery	Classic Mission	Goldwind
Barn Door Furniture	Colonge	Grand Mesa
Barrs Mill Mission	Concord	Grand Mission
Becks Mill	Crossan	Green Gables Furniture
Bentley Furniture	Crown Villa	Greenwich
Birmingham	Dazed	Hampton Bedroom

Hardin Lodge	Mirage	Santa Cruz
Heritage	Miriam	Santa Rosa
Hyland Park	Mission	Savannah
Iron Clad	Modern Shaker	Scottsdale Bedroom
Jackson	Montecito Dining	Scottsdale Dining
Jacob's Mission	Montrose	Sequoia
Kensington	Murphy Wall Bed	Shaker Dining
Keystone Collections	New Albany	Sierra Classic
King Hickory	New England Dining	Stony Brooke Bedroom
Leathercraft	New Haven	Timber Ridge
Levi's Mission	New River Bedroom	Transitions
Liberty Mission	Noah's Mission Bedroom	Tree Crowns Craftsman
Lincoln	North Hampton Dining	Tribeca
Lincoln Avenue	Old English Mission	Valley Shaker
Lincoln Avenue Dining	Platinum	Valley Victorian
Luxembourg	Post Mission	Versailles
Lynnwood	Provence	Victorian
Manhatten	Provincial Cottage	Victorias Tradition
Manor Meyhaus	Redmond Wellington	Voyage Bedroom
Maple Creek	Regal	Warren
Marbella	Richfield	Wellington
Master	Richmond Bedroom	Williamsburg
Master Woodcraft	Richmond Dining	Wind River
Memphis	Rosetta	Winesburg Furniture
Michael's Mission	Rustic Timbers	Worthington
Milan Bedroom	San Juan	

Antiques & Interiors (Main St.)   ★★★

317 North Main Street, High Point, NC, 27260

Hours: Monday-Friday 9:00-5:00,
Saturday 9:00-3:00
Phone: 336-884-4084
Email: info@antint.com
Website: None
Discount: Varies
Payment: VISA, MasterCard, American
Express, Discover, Personal Check
Delivery: White glove delivery

This is the smallest of the four Antiques & Interiors showrooms in High Point, NC. It has a very nice selection of antiques and new furniture at great prices, about 50%-70% off retail. Most of the items here are case goods.

In particular, Antiques & Interiors has beautiful traditional dining room sets from Century, Drexel Heritage, Hickory White, and other high end brands in cherry and mahogany. They also have a nice selection of china cabinets, hutches, bookcases, occasional furniture, and fireplace walls.

This location is nice, but the best store of the four Antiques & Interiors locations is at the old Henredon factory at 615 W. Ward Ave. in High Point. To make the best use of your shopping time, just head straight there.

If you are shopping in High Point, you absolutely must visit the two other locations for Antiques & Interiors, which are much bigger and have an amazing selection!

Vendor carries 8 manufacturer's lines

Bernhardt	Henredon	Kincaid
Century Furniture	Hickory White	Pulaski
Drexel Heritage	Hooker	

Antiques & Interiors (Ward Ave.) ★★★★★

641 W. Ward Ave., High Point, NC, 27260

Hours: Monday-Saturday 9:00-5:00
Phone: 336-885-6255
Email: hpdesigncenter@aol.com
Website: highpointaadc.com
Discount: 50% to 70% off mfr retail
Payment: VISA, MasterCard, American Express, Discover, Personal Check
Delivery: White glove delivery

Do not let the industrial exterior fool you! This store has some of the nicest outlet furniture in the High Point area, and some of the best prices -- 50%-70% off retail!

I used to bring people to this location to shop at the old Henredon factory. I can't believe what Antiques & Interiors has done with this place! I have found so many wonderful things here!

On my most recent visit, I found a beautiful set of six shield-back dining room chairs by Drexel Heritage (pictured on the next page). This set of chairs retailed for $785.00 each, but you could buy this set for $239.00 each! That's a savings of $546.00 per chair, or $3,276.00 on the whole set -- 70% off retail! They looked perfect!

Antiques & Interiors has beautiful traditional dining room sets from Century, Drexel Heritage, Hickory White, and other high end brands in cherry and mahogany. They also have a nice selection of china cabinets, hutches, bookcases, occasional furniture, and fireplace walls. You won't find much upholstery here, but if you're decorating a traditional dining room, living room, or library, this is a great place to shop!

Of the four Antiques & Interiors locations in High Point, this one is the best! To make the best use of your shopping time in High Point, just head straight here!

Drexel Heritage shield-back chairs at Antiques & Interiors

Retail per chair: $785.00 Discounted price per chair: $239.00
Savings at Antiques & Interiors: $546.00 = 70% off retail

Vendor carries 8 manufacturer's lines

Bernhardt	Henredon	Kincaid
Century Furniture	Hickory White	Pulaski
Drexel Heritage	Hooker	

Ashley Interiors

310 S. Elm St., High Point, NC, 27260

Hours: Tuesday-Saturday 9:00-5:00
Phone: 336-889-7573
Email: None
Website: braxtonculler.com
Discount: 50%-75% off mfr retail
Payment: VISA, MasterCard, Personal Check
Delivery: White glove delivery

Ashley Interiors is the Braxton Culler factory outlet. They will take orders by phone or in person for new furniture from Braxton Culler's current line of wicker, rattan, and outdoor furniture at 42%-50% off the manufacturer's suggested retail.

The showroom also has a limited selection of Braxton Culler floor samples and discontinued styles at 75% off retail. These can be purchased by phone if you know exactly what style you want and the outlet happens to have it on the sales floor.

This showroom is closed during April and October due to the semi-annual High Point International Home Furnishings Market, when retailers from all over the U. S. converge on High Point, NC, to see and purchase the latest furniture styles.

However, just prior to closing for market, Ashley Interiors normally has a special sale where all items, including those from Braxton Culler's current line, are marked down to 75% off retail. These sales normally run for the entire months of March and September. Please check my web site, www.smartdecorating.com, for the exact sale dates each spring and fall.

Vendor carries 1 manufacturer's lines

Braxton Culler

Baker Odds & Ends (Kohler)

★★★★★

765-J Woodlake Rd., Kohler, WI, 53044

Hours: Monday-Friday 10:00-6:00,
Saturday 10:00-5:00, Sunday12:00-5:00
Phone: 920-458-2033
Email: See Web site
Website: kohlerinteriors.com
Discount: 60%-75% off mfr retail
Payment: VISA, MasterCard, American
Express, Personal Check
Delivery: Limited third party shipping

Baker Odds & Ends in Kohler, WI, was the first of Baker Furniture's new "Odds and Ends" outlets where they sell direct to the public. Baker is owned by the Kohler Co., which is based here. Most of the items here are in first quality condition and sell for 60%-75% off retail.

The outlet has a good variety of upholstered pieces, beds, desks, armoires, chests, etc. Most pieces are floor samples from the various Baker wholesale showrooms in design centers around the U. S. Some are overruns from their manufacturing plants in nearby Holland, MI, and Grand Rapids, MI.

A separate company, Jim's Delivery, makes deliveries from this outlet to Chicago and various points in Indiana and Michigan. Please call (920) 565-3738 for more information. Other customers must make their own arrangements to take purchases home.

New pieces arrive every Wednesday. If you're going to be in the Milwaukee or Madison area, you should definitely consider taking a side trip to this outlet.

Vendor carries 1 manufacturer's lines

Baker Furniture

Bassett Furniture Factory Outlet ★★★★★

115 East Church Street, Martinsville, VA, 24112

Hours: Monday-Friday 10:00-6:00,
Saturday 9:00-5:00
Phone: 276-638-2040
Email: hookeroutlet@hotmail.com
Website: bassettfurniture.com
Discount: 60%-70% off mfr retail
Payment: VISA, MasterCard, Personal
Check
Delivery: White glove delivery

Bassett Furniture has recently moved its only factory outlet to a new location in downtown Martinsville, VA. Please note that the Bassett Factory Outlet's longtime location next to the home office on Fairystone Parkway in Bassett, VA is now closed.

The new Bassett Factory Outlet is owned by Fred Martin Associates, and managed by my good friend Tim Martin (above). He also manages the factory outlets for Hooker, Century, Lane, and Dar Lee Furniture, all in the same city block. Discounts begin at 65% and up on Bassett Furniture here.

On a recent trip, I found a great deal on a complete queen bedroom set in first quality condition from Bassett Furniture's 5th Avenue Collection. The bed retails for $1,299.00 at Bassett Furniture's website, with a clearance price from Bassett Furniture of $979.00, a discount of 25% off retail.

However, if you had gone to the Bassett Furniture Factory Outlet on the very same day the prices above appeared at Bassett Furniture's web site, you could have purchased the 5th Avenue queen bed pictured on the next page for only $599.00, a discount of 54% off Bassett Furniture's retail, a whopping 39% cheaper than the "clearance" price listed at Bassett Furniture's corporate website. Clearly, it pays to shop in person!

The rest of the bedroom set (dresser, chest, nightstands, etc.) could be purchased at similar deep discounts, also in new first-quality condition.

The staff here is great to work with. You will not find a friendlier or more helpful place to buy furniture. I highly recommend this source.

5th Avenue Panel Bed at the Bassett Furniture Factory Outlet

Retail: $1,299.00 Discounted price: $599.00
Savings at the Bassett Furniture Factory Outlet: $700.00 = 54% off retail

Bedroom & Mattress Discounters ★

1000-A North Main St., High Point, NC, 27262

Hours: Monday-Saturday 10:00-6:00
Phone: / 800-503-1053
Email: info@ncfurnitureman.com
Website: ncfurnitureman.com
Discount: 40%-50% off mfr retail
Payment: VISA, MasterCard, Discover, Personal Check
Delivery: Full service in-home delivery and set-up

This business has a convoluted, and scary, history. Bedroom & Mattress Discounters (aka www.ncfurnitureman.com, aka www.ncfactorydirect.com, aka Dean Sechrest) opened in 2004 in downtown High Point. It was a very small showroom, without much furniture on display. The picture above was taken in 2005. The physical store was closed and vacant as of 2009.

The web site and phone number for this company remain active, and presumably they are still accepting orders, even though the physical address listed at the website (shown above) has been vacant for years. Another company is also registered to the same owner: NC Factory Direct, aka www.ncfactorydirect.com.

This company is not "factory direct". The owner has used multiple names over the last few years. The physical address given at company's website is a vacant building. Clearly, it's not a reputable company. Don't shop here.

Vendor carries 5 manufacturer's lines

Beautyrest	Homelegance	Thermo-Sleep
Elliotts Designs	Simmons	

Bernhardt Factory Outlet ★★★★★

Manufacturer-Owned Factory Outlets, 4916 Hickory Blvd, Hickory, NC, 28601

Hours: Tuesday-Saturday 9:00-6:00
Phone: 828-313-0795
Email: outlet@bernhardt.com
Website: bernhardt.com
Discount: 55%-70% off mfr retail
Payment: VISA, MasterCard, Discover, Personal Check
Delivery: White glove delivery

This is Bernhardt's only factory outlet nationwide. It's on the north side of Hickory, not far from their factory. The outlet itself is fairly large and has a good selection of upholstery and case goods at 50%-60% off retail. Please note that they've recently changed their hours. They are no longer open on Mondays.

This is a particularly good outlet to visit if you're looking for medium quality contemporary furniture, which can be hard to find at U. S. factory outlets. They had a nice selection of contemporary upholstery and case goods, in addition to many more traditional styles.

On a recent visit, I saw a nice sofa and chair set that is very similar to Bernhardt's popular Davian sofa (pictured on the next page). The only difference is that the Davian sofa does not have welt cord on the edges, where the sofa in the outlet did.

Bernhardt's Davian sofa retails for $1,700.00 at Outrageous Interiors and other sources, but you could buy this sofa at the Bernhardt Factory Outlet in new first quality condition for only $499.00, a savings of $1,201.00 or 71% off retail! The matching chair was available for only $299.00.

Virtually all of the furniture in stock is first-quality, although there are a few seconds and irregulars. Make sure you look each piece over very carefully because, unlike most outlets, Bernhardt does not use special coded tags to mark pieces that have flaws or damage.

Bernhardt has made arrangements with local refinisher Highland Woodcraft to correct any flaws or damage for $50.00-$150.00, depending on the specific job that needs to be done. Work is normally competed in 1-2 weeks, but it can take as long as a month during periods of heavy demand.

This small outlet mall also houses factory owned outlets for Caracole, Kincaid and La-Z-Boy.

These outlets hold an after market sale twice each year in early May and early November when prices are discounted even more than usual. Please check www.smartdecorating.com for current sale dates. If you're in the Hickory area, this outlet should definitely be on your "must-visit" list.

Bernhardt sofa at the Bernhardt Factory Outlet

Comparable retail: $1,700.00 Discounted price: $499.00
Savings at the Bernhardt Factory Outlet: $1,201.00 = 71% off retail

Vendor carries 1 manufacturer's lines

Bernhardt

Boulevard Bazaar

★★★★★

3021 Griffith St., Charlotte, NC, 28203

Hours: Friday-Saturday 10:00-5:00,
Sunday12:00-5:00
Phone: 704-527-4223
Email: Questions@boulevardbazaar.com
Website: boulevardbazaar.com
Discount: 45%-65% off mfr retail
Payment: VISA, MasterCard, Personal
Check
Delivery: White glove delivery

Boulevard Bazaar in Charlotte, NC was bought out by Kelly McGrath, president of Hollin Gate in Granite Falls, NC. All of the services and furniture formerly available at the Charlotte store are now available from Hollin Gate, which is just north of Hickory, NC.

I've known Kelly McGrath for many years. He's been in the wholesale furniture industry for a very long time. His stores have excellent customer service.

Please see the review of Hollin Gate in this book for further details.

Boyles Furniture ★★★★

182 Farmington Road, Mocksville, NC, 27028

Hours: Monday-Saturday 9:00-5:30
Phone: 888-848-4551 / 888-848-4551
Email: helpdesk@boylesfurniture.com
Website: boyles.com
Discount: 20%-40% off mfr retail
Delivery: Full service in-home delivery and set-up. Customer pays freight company directly for shipping costs

Boyles Furniture has reopened at its original flagship store in Mocksville, NC. They had excellent service for many years at their former Hickory locations, so it's good to see them back.

Their prices on brand new special order furniture are typically 30%-40% off retail. Most of the brands carried are very high end: Baker, Drexel-Heritage, Century, Henkel Harris, and Hekman, among many others.

Boyles also has good deals on discontinued items in their "Back Room". Discontinued items are typically in new condition here, and discounts run from 60%-70% off retail.

On a recent visit, I found this bargain on this "Little Joe" leather chair and ottoman from Century, pictured on the next page. Century's retail on this chair and ottoman is $7,860.00. Boyles can special order this item new in any color for $4,700.00, a discount of 40% off retail. You can buy this one of a kind floor sample in excellent condition from Boyles "Back Room" for only $2,499.00, a discount of 68% off retail! It had no flaws I could see.

Boyles is right off I-40 between Hickory and High Point. If you plan a furniture shopping trip to either city, you should definitely stop in at Boyles!

"Little Joe" chair and ottoman
from Century Furniture at Boyles

Retail: $7,860.00 Discounted price: $2,499.00
Savings at Boyles: $5,361.00 = 68% off retail

Vendor carries 23 manufacturer's lines

Baker Furniture
Better Homes
Century Furniture
Coastal Living
Craftmaster Furniture
Drexel Heritage
Ferguson Copeland
Four Hands

Guardsman
Habersham
Hancock & Moore
Harden
Henkel Harris
Henredon
Jackson Carter
Leathercraft

Padma's Plantation
Paula Deen Home
Pennsylvania House
Rugs by Naja
Stanley
Universal Furniture
Uttermost

Brass Bed Shoppe   ★★★

13800 Miles Avenue, Cleveland Heights, OH, 44105

Hours: Monday-Saturday 10:00-6:00
Phone: 216-371-0400
Email: bedshoppe@aol.com
Website: brassbedshoppe.com
Discount: 50% off mfr retail
Payment: VISA, MasterCard, Personal Check
Delivery: All orders are shipped by common carrier with assembly required

The Brass Bed Shoppe is a true factory outlet. They manufacture their own line of brass and iron beds and sell them at about 50% off retail. The quality is very good, and they have a nice selection of traditional styles.

They also carry beds by many other makers, including Wesley Allen, Corsican, and Elliott's Designs, just to name a few. They do not publish any comprehensive lists of the lines they carry. Please inquire directly if there is a certain brass or iron bed on which you would like to compare their prices.

Please be aware that this source ships via common carrier, and beds will require assembly. Assembly of these types of beds is not difficult, and should not be a problem for most people. Typical delivery fees are $65.00 to $95.00 for each bed, depending on how far away you live from their warehouse in Ohio.

Brass Bed Shoppe has a good record with the BBB considering the amount of business they do. As of this writing in March 2016, they have only two complaints in the last three years, with no complaints during the last twelve months. I consider them a reliable source.

Vendor carries 3 manufacturer's lines

Corsican Furniture   Elliotts Designs   Wesley Allen

Broyhill Factory Outlet

★★★★★

Manufacturer-Owned Factory Outlets, 4930 Hickory Blvd, Hickory, NC, 28601

Hours: Monday-Saturday 9:00-6:00
Phone: 828-758-8899
Email: None
Website: broyhillfurniture.com
Discount: 45%-60% off mfr retail
Payment: VISA, MasterCard, American Express, Personal Check
Delivery: White glove delivery

Broyhill Furniture closed their only factory outlet on February 22nd, 2014. Please check my website, www.smartdecorating.com, for news on any new sources for Broyhill outlet furniture.

Vendor carries 1 manufacturer's lines

Broyhill

Bulluck Furniture Company ★★★

124 S. Church Street, Rocky Mount, NC, 27804

Hours: Monday-Friday 9:00-5:30,
Saturday 9:00-5:00
Phone: 252-446-1138
Email: None
Website: bulluckfurniture.com
Discount: 30%-50% off mfr retail
Payment: VISA, MasterCard, Discover,
Personal Check
Delivery: White glove delivery nationwide

Bulluck Furniture has been in business since 1900, and they have a lovely showroom in Rocky Mount, NC, about an hour's drive east of Raleigh on Hwy. 64. They have good deals by phone on all the lines below.

In early January each year, they hold a huge furniture clearance sale. Then in late January and throughout February, they hold huge accessory clearance sales each weekend. Check www.smartdecorating.com for exact dates and times.

I've never heard a single complaint about this company, and their record with the Better Business Bureau is spotless. I would certainly recommend them as a reputable source. If you're in the Rocky Mount area, definitely check out the sales. If you're ordering furniture by phone, call them for a comparison price.

Vendor carries 77 manufacturer's lines

Allibert	Creative Metal & Wood	Henkel Harris
Amotek/USA	Dixie	Henry Link
Barcalounger	Ello	Hickory Chair
Bevan-Funnell	Fairington	High Point Furniture
Bradington Young	Ficks Reed	Hooker
Carolina Mirror	Finkel Outdoor	Howard Miller
Carver's Guild	Fremarc Designs	Hyundai Furniture
Classics by Casabique	Friedman Brothers	J. B. Ross
Colonial Traditions	Garcia Imports	Jamestown Sterling
Councill	Gregson	Jasper Cabinet
Craftique	Habersham	Jeffco
Cramer	Hancock & Moore	Jofco

John Boos & Co.	O'Asian	Tomlin Lamps
John-Richard	Pleion	Tradition House
Lane	Pompeii	Tramswall
Laneventure	Royal Patina	Trosby Furniture
Lexington	Schott	Venture By Lane
Link Taylor	Shelby Williams	Vogue Rattan
Lloyd/Flanders	Southampton	Wesley Hall
Lone Star Leather	Southwood	Wicker World
Madison Square	St. Timothy	Winston
Maitland-Smith	Stanley	Woodfield
McGuire	Stanton Cooper	Woodmark Furniture
Meadowcraft	Statesville Chair	Wright Table
Michael Thomas	Stewart	Young Hinkle
National Mt. Airy	Telescope	

CAPA

★★★

319 N Main St, High Point, NC, 27262

Hours: Monday-Saturday 9:00-5:00
Phone: 336-885-9999
Email: None
Website: capaimports.com
Discount: Importer direct to public
Payment: VISA, MasterCard, Personal Check
Delivery: White glove delivery

CAPA Imports has been on Main St. in High Point for a number of years. They sell imported furniture, rugs, pillows, and accessories directly to the public and to designers nationwide.

Some of their furniture is traditional, but most of their stock has an Oriental or Middle Eastern look. They have some very nice kilim pillows and rugs, for instance.

If you are in High Point, you might want to check out some of the accessories and occasional furniture here.

Carolina Chair

★★★★★

1822 Brian Dr, Conover, NC, 28613-8852

Hours: Monday-Friday 9:00-5:00
Phone: None / 800-653-9757
Email: info@carolinachair.com
Website: carolinachair.com
Discount: Factory direct to the public
Payment: VISA, MasterCard, Discover
Delivery: Free nationwide white glove delivery

Carolina Chair is a terrific factory direct source for high quality upholstery direct to the public. All of their upholstered furniture is eight-way hand-tied with steel coil springs, double doweled, glued and screwed, corner blocked, with hardwood frames. Upholstery manufacturing does not get better than this.

It's worth noting as well that they ship nationwide free of charge with full white glove indoor delivery service. That is unusual and should be taken into account when comparing their prices.

I visited their factory in Conover, NC, and they really are manufacturer direct to the public. Their factory floor was bustling with activity. They have a nice range of styles, colors, fabrics, and leather at their web site above.

The owners, Cathy and H. D. Fry are the third generation of furniture manufacturers in their family. Their grandfather, H. D. Fry Sr., founded Hickory-Fry Furniture in 1926. This brother-sister team grew up around furniture manufacturing. I grew up in a home furnishings factory, too, and I can tell you there is no better way to learn about quality.

All pieces can be customized to order. The photo on the next page shows a custom leather and fabric sectional sofa with ottoman that had just been completed the day of my visit. The final cost was $7,000.00 which is amazing for that level of quality in a completely custom, one of a kind product, especially when it includes free shipping.

The factory is not open to shoppers, but they will see customers by appointment. Their website is very comprehensive, and offers the easiest way to buy their product. Processing sales via a website rather than maintaining a retail showroom is also one of the ways Carolina Chair keeps its prices low.

Please understand that this is a working factory. There are no retail salespeople or showroom samples on display. All of their furniture is custom order. There are no outlet items on display for immediate purchase.

However, if you have a large or complex project you wish to discuss in person, you are invited to call the factory for an appointment.

The staff and owners are very helpful and professional. I also like the fact that the people taking your order are on site at the factory itself, which makes quick and accurate communication about your order much easier. I highly recommend this source!

Custom leather sectional at the Carolina Chair factory

Wholesale price to the public: $7,000.00

Carolina Furniture Outlet

★★

3516 Springs Rd. NE, Hickory, NC, 28601

Hours: Monday-Saturday 10:00-5:00
Phone: 828-256-3456
Email: Robin@CarolinaFurnitureOutlet.com
Website: carolinafurnitureoutlet.com
Discount: 30%-50% off mfr retail
Payment: VISA, MasterCard, Discover, Personal Check
Delivery: Store delivers in local area

Carolina Furniture Outlet buys closeouts from local factories and sells them in a small store about 15 minutes north of downtown Hickory, NC. Their showroom is very small. They carry odds and ends from a variety of middle end manufacturers: Lane, Signature, and other random brands.

Their prices are no better than the much larger outlets for the same furniture brands in the main shopping areas around Hickory, NC. For instance, on a recent visit here, I found a leather recliner rocker by Lane priced at $499.00 (pictured on the next page). They only had the one recliner on display, without its matching sofa or loveseat.

Coffey Furniture in nearby Granite Falls has hundreds of comparable leather rockers from Lane and La-Z-Boy priced around $479.00, plus most of them can be purchased with matching sofas and loveseats. No item number was given for the recliner at Carolina Furniture Outlet, but the typical retail on leather recliners of this type is about $1,000.00.

This is not a good destination for out of town furniture shoppers. It's at least a 30 minute round trip from the Hickory Furniture Mart, and it just isn't worth the travel time. You can find equivalent deals at much more convenient locations in Hickory.

Vendor carries 2 manufacturer's lines

Lane   Signature Designs

Lane recliner at Carolina Furniture Outlet

Retail: $1,000.00 Discounted price: $499.00
Savings at Carolina Furniture Outlet: $501.00 = 50% off retail

Carolina Interiors

115 Oak Ave., Kannapolis, NC, 28081

Hours: Monday-Friday 10:00-5:00,
Saturday 10:00-4:00
Phone: 704-933-3333
Email: sales@carolina-interiors.com
Website: carolina-interiors.com
Discount: 30%-60% off manufacturers
suggested retail
Payment: Personal Check
Delivery: White glove delivery

Carolina Interiors in Cannon Village has reopened under new management. The new owner, Joel Blackwelder, has no affiliation with the former owners of Carolina Interiors, K-Town Furniture Inc. K-Town Furniture left a lot of unhappy customers when they went out of business several years ago.

The new Carolina Interiors is doing very well by their customers. They have a spotless record with the BBB, with no complaints they opened in 2010.

They offer white glove delivery nationwide, and their prices are very competitive. I recommend calling them for a quote.

Vendor carries 36 manufacturer's lines

A-America	Global Views, Inc.	Lillian August
A.P. Generations	Hancock & Moore	Magnussen Home
American Drew	Harden	Palliser
Baker Furniture	Hekman	Randall-Allan
Bassett Mirror	Hickory Heritage	Sligh
Casa Fiora	Hickory White	Southwood
CTH Sherrill Occasional	Jamison	Stanley
Curations Limited	Jessica Charles	Summer Classics
Currey & Co.	Jonathan Charles	Uttermost
Designmaster	Kalaty Rugs	Vanguard Furniture
Drexel Heritage	Kincaid	Wildwood Lamps
Fine Art Lamps	Lexington	Woodbridge

Carolina Patio Warehouse ★★★

58 Largo Dr., Stamford, CT, 06907

Hours: Monday-Saturday 9:00-6:00
Phone: 203-975-9939 / 800-672-8466
Email: See Web site
Website: patio.com
Discount: 30%-60% off mfr retail
Payment: VISA, MasterCard, American Express, Discover, Personal Check
Delivery: White glove and UPS delivery

Carolina Patio Warehouse isn't actually based in North Carolina. It was purchased a few years ago by Patio.com, which owns twelve patio stores in Virginia, Connecticut, New York, Maryland, Massachusetts, and Pennsylvania.

Carolina Patio Warehouse/Patio.com has a written guarantee promising to beat any competitors prices on wicker, rattan, and outdoor furniture.

Their prices are generally about 30%-60% below the manufacturer's suggested retail. Shipping runs about 9% of the purchase price with a minimum shipping charge of $65.00 on truck shipments, and $25 on UPS shipments.

Vendor carries 29 manufacturer's lines

Atlantic Bench	Kingsley-Bate	Telescope
Basta Sole by Tropitone	Laneventure	Triconfort
Beka	Lyon Shaw	Tropitone
Casual Creations	Outdoor Classics	Tye-Sil Patio
Colonial Castings	Pawley's Island	Veneman
Coppa	Polywood	Venture By Lane
Cushion Factory	Prairie Leisure	Windsor Design
Galtech	Samsonite Aluminum	Windward Classics
Homecrest	Scanply	Zip
Kettler	Summer Classics	

Catawba Furniture Mall

★★★

377 US Highway 70 SW, Hickory, NC, 28602

Hours: Monday-Saturday 10:00-6:00
Phone: 828-324-9701
Email: info@catawbafurniture.com
Website: www.catawbafurnituremall.com

As of September 2013, The Catawba Furniture Mall in Hickory, NC, has closed permanently.

If you were planning to visit, please consider visiting the nearby Hickory Furniture Mart instead. They have great deals!

Cedar Rock Home Furnishings   ★★

3483 Hickory Blvd.,,, Hwy. 321 S., Hudson, NC, 28638

Hours: Monday-Saturday 9:00-6:00
Phone: 828-396-2361
Email: info@cedarrockfurniture.com
Website: cedarrockfurniture.com
Discount: 40%-50% off mfr retail
Payment: VISA, MasterCard, Discover, Personal Check
Delivery: White glove delivery

Cedar Rock Home Furnishings is located in Hudson, NC, about 20 minutes north of the main furniture shopping area in Hickory, NC. They have a very nice selection of medium quality lines, including Lexington, Broyhill, Stanley, and Hooker. They've been in business for over 20 years.

Their prices run 20% to 40% off retail. For instance, on a recent visit I found a Broyhill #6544 "McKinney" sofa on sale (pictured on the next page) This sofa retails for $1238.00, but you could special order it from Cedar Rock in any color for $949.00, a discount of $249.00 or about 25% off retail. You could buy the floor sample sofa pictured for only $799.00, a savings of $35% off retail.

That's not a great deal. The Broyhill Factory Outlet is much closer to Hickory, NC, and they had similar Broyhill sofa sets for about 50% off retail.

If you're special ordering Broyhill, American Drew, Hammary, or any of the other lines I saw here, you will likely find better pricing at Hickory Park in the Hickory Furniture Mart. I would definitely shop around for better pricing before placing any special orders here.

Broyhill sofa at Cedar Rock Home Furnishings

Retail: $1,238.00 Discounted price: $799.00
Savings at Cedar Rock Home Furnishings: $439.00 = 35% off retail

Vendor carries 32 manufacturer's lines

American Drew	Hammary	Mobel
Bassett	Hekman	Omnia Leather
Bassett Baby/Juvenile	Hickory Chair	Palliser
Braxton Culler	Hickory Classics	Pulaski
Broyhill	Homelegance	Riverside Furniture
Butler Specialty	Howard Miller	Schnadig
Clayton Marcus	Lea Industries	Stein World
CMI - Colonial Mills	Legacy Classic	Thomasville
Crawford of Jamestown	Liberty	Vineyard Furniture
Fairmont Designs	Magnussen Home	Wesley Allen
Furniture Traditions	Master Design	

Classic Furniture ★

2052 Highway U.S. 321 South, Lenoir, NC, 28645

Hours: Monday-Saturday 10:00-6:00
Phone: 828-726-8880
Email: None
Website: None
Discount: Factory direct to public
Payment: Personal Check
Delivery: Full service in-home delivery and set-up. Customer pays freight company directly for shipping costs

Classic Furniture advertises a line of custom casegoods to the public. Their showroom is small and unremarkable, frankly. The furniture is solidly made in classic traditional styles, but there is nothing here to set them apart as to price or styling. The drive to the showroom will take you considerably out of the way from the main outlet areas, and it really isn't worth the travel time.

They have stopped advertising on their web site that they can special order other brands, in fact, as of this writing in March 2016, the web site is totally offline. They will still offer to special order other brands to walk in customers, but I would not take them up on it. It would be safer to stick with discounters who have furniture on display from the special order brand in which you are interested. Having a catalog on display does not make you an authorized dealer.

Classic Furniture does not take credit cards, so you will not have much recourse if your furniture does not arrive in good shape when you get back home.

There are better sources in the area for this type of furniture, with better reputations for service. Amish Oak & Cherry at the Hickory Furniture Mart is a safer bet to order this type of furniture for delivery out of state.

Club Furniture

★★★★

11535 Carmel Commons Blvd., Suite 202, Charlotte, NC, 28226

Hours: Monday-Friday 9:00-5:00
Phone: None / 888-378-8383
Email: clubinfo@onesourceplus.com
Website: clubfurniture.com
Discount: 10%-40% off comparable brands
Payment: VISA, MasterCard, American Express, Discover
Delivery: Full service in-home delivery and set-up. Most items ship free.

Club Furniture at clubfurniture.com sells private label upholstered furniture comparable to Pottery Barn, Restoration Hardware, Williams Sonoma, Crate & Barrel, Mitchell Gold, and similar lines. Club Furniture's prices are 20%-40% less, though.

For example, Pottery Barn offers their "Manhattan" Club Chair in their basic leather for $1,564.00 including shipping. Club Furniture has a nearly identical "Parker" club chair for only $1,295.20 including shipping as of this writing in February 2016. That is a 16% savings!

I cannot find any real difference between the manufacturing methods used on upholstered furniture by ClubFurniture.com (made at several North Carolina factories) and Pottery Barn (which is actually made in Taylorsville, NC by Mitchell Gold). So, why pay more for the heavily advertised name, glitzy catalogs, and high rent store at the mall?

ClubFurniture.com keeps their prices low by selling via the web only. They have no showrooms open to the public. I have met the owners and inspected samples of their furniture personally, though, and I have to say I am impressed. All of their upholstered furniture is made in the U. S. Their case goods are imported, as are most case goods sold in the U. S. today.

They do offer free swatches, which is nice. Many special order companies charge. They run sales from time to time for as much as 15% off their regular pricing. They also have a small clearance section on the web site to sell off the very few items that are ever returned. Returns make up less than 1% of their sales.

Customers order online. Furniture is custom manufactured to order within 4-6 weeks. Then, when the furniture is ready, the customer is asked to pay for the furniture and shipping in full when the furniture is ready to be shipped to the customer. This is also a generous policy in the industry. Most special order furniture sellers require a non-refundable deposit before they will begin work on your order.

Club Furniture has had an excellent record with the Better Business Bureau during the ten years they have been in business. As of this writing, they have an A+ record with the BBB with only two resolved complaints within the last three years.

Their return policy is one of the most generous in the special order furniture industry: keep your new furniture for up to 30 days. If you still are not happy, return it. Club Furniture pays freight both ways and deducts only a 10% restocking fee. Very few special order furniture companies accept returns for any reason. I highly recommend this source!

Leather chair from Club Furniture

Club Furniture price: $1,295.20
Pottery Barn price for nearly identical chair: $1,549.00
Savings at Club Furniture: $254.00 = 16% off Pottery Barn price

Coffey Furniture ★★★★★

4453 Hickory Blvd., Granite Falls, NC, 28630

Hours: Monday-Saturday 8:30-5:00, Sunday 1:00-5:00
Phone: 828-396-2900
Email: info@coffeyfurniturenc.com
Website: None
Discount: 30%-60% off mfr retail
Payment: VISA, MasterCard, Personal Check
Delivery: White glove delivery

Coffey Furniture specializes in purchasing market samples from the various wholesale trade shows and reselling them to the public. They have three huge warehouses filled with all kinds of case goods and upholstery. They will also special order new furniture from many lines.

I found some great bargains during my most recent visit, like this "Rave" entertainment console from Hammary (pictured on the next page). This item retailed for $999.00 before it was discontinued, but you could buy this piece in first quality condition at Coffey Furniture for only $599.00, a savings of 40% off retail!

Coffey Furniture has a wide selection of new and sample case goods for every room: bedroom, dining room, occasional, and outdoor.

Coffey Furniture also has a huge selection of upholstery samples and discontinued styles, most of which come in complete sofa/loveseat/chair sets. They have a large section devoted entirely to La-A-Boy samples and closeouts in first quality condition. The prices on La-Z-Boy furniture at Coffey Furniture were better than the prices at the La-Z-Boy Factory Outlet five minutes down the road!

The prices I have observed here seem to run approximately 40% to 60% off retail. Coffey Furniture has a spotless reputation with the BBB, and I've never heard a single reader complaint about them either.

If you're in the Hickory area, it's worth the 15 minute drive north on Hwy. 321 to check out Coffey Furniture. I highly recommend this source!

Hammary "Rave" entertainment center at Coffey Furniture

Retail: $999.00 Discounted price: $599.00
Savings at Coffey Furniture: $400.00 = 40% off retail

Vendor carries 61 manufacturer's lines

Action by Lane	Fairfield Chair	Morganton Chair
American Drew	Fairmont Designs	Ohio Table Pad
Athens	Fashion Bed Group	Parker Southern
Bassett	Flexsteel	Peters-Revington
Bassett Baby/Juvenile	Goodwin Weavers	Philip Reinisch
Berkline	Hickory Hill	Pulaski
Berkshire	Hickory Mark	Ridgeway Clocks
Best Chair	Holiday House Sleepers	Rowe Furniture
Blacksmith Shop	Howard Miller	Royale Komfort Bedding
Cal-Style	Hyundai Furniture	Seay
Century Rugs	J. B. Ross	South Sea Rattan
Chatham County	Kimball	Spring Air
Chromcraft	Lane	Stein World
Clayton Marcus	Laneventure	Temple
Cochrane Furniture	Largo	U. S. Furniture
Crawford of Jamestown	Lea Industries	Universal Furniture
Denny Lamps	Legacy Classic	Vanguard Pictures
Dining Ala Carte	Liberty	Venture By Lane
Dresher	Link Taylor	Wesley Allen
Earth & Elements	Lloyd/Flanders	
England Corsair	Magnussen Home	

Colfax Furniture (Greensboro) ★

3614 S. Holden Road, Greensboro, NC, 27407

Hours: Monday-Friday 10:00-8:00,
Saturday 10:00-6:00, Sunday1:00-6:00
Phone: 336-855-0498
Email: None
Website: colfaxfurniture.net
Discount: 40%-60% off mfr retail
Payment: VISA, MasterCard, Discover,
Personal Check
Delivery: Local delivery only

Colfax Furniture advertises that they offer market samples, closeouts, and discontinued styles directly to the public. In reality, I found very few market samples or discontinued styles during my most recent visit to all of their stores.

The vast majority of the case goods and upholstery I found here were "special buys", discounted styles in current production that you can also find in other stores and on the internet at similar prices.

For instance, all of the Colfax stores I visited had this sofa (pictured on the next page), "Montgomery" by Ashley Furniture. Colfax offered this sofa for $451.99, a savings of 47% off of the retail price of $849.99. This does not include shipping costs.

You can find the identical sofa cheaper at other sources. MathisBrothers.com, the website for the Mathis Brothers brick and mortar furniture store chain in Oklahoma and California, offers the identical sofa in any color for only $410.95, a savings of 50% off the retail price from Ashley.

There's nothing special about the "special buys" at Colfax Furniture. It's just like thousands of other cheap furniture stores nationwide. There are much better sources in North Carolina that really do give great deals on closeouts, discontinued styles, and market samples.

Ashley sofa at Colfax Furniture

Retail: $849.99 Discounted price: $451.99
Savings at Colfax Furniture: $398.00 = 47% off retail

Vendor carries 20 manufacturer's lines

American Woodcrafters

Ashley Furniture

Best Home Furnishings

Catnapper

Coaster Fine Furniture

Crown Mark Furniture

Fusion Designs

Homelegance

Jackson Furniture

Lane

Largo

Legacy Classic

Millennium

Powell

Pulaski

Signature Designs

Simmons

Standard

Stein World

Tennessee Enterprises

Colfax Furniture (Winston-Salem) ★

801 Silas Creek Parkway, Winston-Salem, NC, 27127

Hours: Monday-Friday 10:00-8:00,
Saturday 10:00-6:00, Sunday1:00-6:00
Phone: 336-499-0915
Email: None
Website: colfaxfurniture.com
Discount: 40%-60% off mfr retail
Payment: VISA, MasterCard, Discover,
Personal Check
Delivery: Local delivery only

Colfax Furniture advertises that they offer market samples, closeouts, and discontinued styles directly to the public. This location has a large sign promising savings of "up to 73%". In reality, I found very few market samples or discontinued styles during my most recent visit to all of their stores.

The vast majority of the case goods and upholstery I found here were "special buys", discounted styles in current production that you can also find in other stores and on the internet at similar prices.

For instance, all of the Colfax stores I visited had this oversized chair (pictured on the next page), "Richland" by Ashley Furniture. Colfax offered this chair for $567.99, a savings of 47% off of the retail price of $1,079.99. This does not include shipping costs.

You can find the identical chair cheaper from other sources. Furniturecart.com offers the identical chair for $499.25 with free shipping, a savings of 54% off the retail price from Ashley.

There's nothing special about the "special buys" at Colfax Furniture. It's just like thousands of other cheap furniture stores nationwide. There are much better sources in North Carolina that really do give great deals on closeouts, discontinued styles, and market samples.

Ashley chair at Colfax Furniture

Retail: $1,079.99 Discounted price: $567.99
Savings at Colfax Furniture: $512.00 = 47% off retail

Vendor carries 20 manufacturer's lines

American Woodcrafters	Homelegance	Pulaski
Ashley Furniture	Jackson Furniture	Signature Designs
Best Home Furnishings	Lane	Simmons
Catnapper	Largo	Standard
Coaster Fine Furniture	Legacy Classic	Stein World
Crown Mark Furniture	Millennium	Tennessee Enterprises
Fusion Designs	Powell	

Colfax Furniture Clearance Center ★

1108 East Mountain St., Kernersville, NC, 27284

Hours: Monday-Saturday 10:00-6:00, Sunday1:00-6:00
Phone: 336-855-0498
Email: Please see company website
Website: colfaxfurniture.com
Discount: 40% to 60% off mfr retail
Payment: VISA, MasterCard, Personal Check
Delivery: Local delivery only

Colfax Furniture Clearance Center advertises "Up to 75% off retail on market samples, closeouts, and discontinueds". They carry low to medium quality case goods and upholstery from Simmons, Aspenhome, and Harden Manufacturing (a cheap brand out of Alabama, not the high-end Harden Furniture from New York).

Overall, I find their quality, selection, and pricing disappointing. I saw very few market samples. I saw the same basic selection of sofas, chairs, and bedroom sets in all three Greensboro area Colfax stores during my most recent visit. Most of the brands and styles here are currently available at stores and websites nationwide at similar prices. There was nothing special to be found here in the way or market sample bargains or deals.

For instance, on a recent visit I found a "Cambridge" queen bedroom set from Aspenhome on sale (pictured on the next page). It's listed as a "five piece set", but if we look at the tag, we see that three of the pieces are all parts of the bed. I can't remember ever seeing a furniture store list the headboard, footboard, and side rails as three pieces of a bedroom set instead of just one.

The retail given on the tag for this set (bed, dresser, mirror) is $3,789.99, with a discounted price of $1,997.00, which is a savings of $1,792.99 or 47% off retail. This is far more typical of the discounts I saw here. Most were in the 40%-60% off range, not the 75% in their ads.

There are other sources for Aspenhome that offer a better grouping of the same bedroom set with a queen bed, mirror, nightstand, and a larger dresser for only $2,166.00.

This isn't much of a clearance center, and it certainly isn't worth driving there in person. Shoppers from out of state should focus their limited shopping time on the clearance centers in the area that have much better selection and pricing on market samples and discontinued styles.

Aspenhome bedroom set at Colfax Furniture Clearance Center

Retail: $3,789.99 Discounted price: $1,997.00
Savings at Colfax Furniture Clearance Center: $1,792.99 = 47% off retail

Vendor carries 20 manufacturer's lines

American Woodcrafters	Homelegance	Pulaski
Ashley Furniture	Jackson Furniture	Signature Designs
Best Home Furnishings	Lane	Simmons
Catnapper	Largo	Standard
Coaster Fine Furniture	Legacy Classic	Stein World
Crown Mark Furniture	Millennium	Tennessee Enterprises
Fusion Designs	Powell	

Contempo Concepts

206 West 4th St., Winston-Salem, NC

Hours: Monday-Friday 10:00-6:00,
Saturday 10:00-5:00
Phone: 336-723-1717
Email: jim@contempoconcepts.com
Website: contempoconcepts.com
Discount: Up to 60% off mfr retail
Payment: VISA, MasterCard, Discover,
Personal Check
Delivery: Free delivery nationwide

Contempo Concetps closed their beautiful Winston-Salem store in late 2014, citing a lack of foot traffic. They announced at the time that they would continue their website, www.contempoconcepts.com, as an online furniture seller.

Since then, the website has also shut down. Contempo Concepts appears to be permanently out of business.

Darlee Factory Outlet

★★★★★

105 East Church St., Martinsville, VA, 24112

Hours: Monday-Saturday 10:00-6:00
Phone: 276-638-2040
Email: hookeroutlet@hotmail.com
Website: None
Discount: 50%-75% off mfr retail
Payment: VISA, MasterCard, American Express, Discover, Personal Check
Delivery: White glove delivery

The Darlee Outdoor Furniture Factory Outlet is owned by the Martin family, who also own and operate the factory outlets here for Hooker, Bassett, and Lane, as well as Martin Plaza and The Showroom. Please see individual listings in this book for detailed information on all of these other sources.

Tim Martin is the primary manager of Martin Plaza and all of the factory outlets owned by the Martin family. Please email him above with any product questions.

Unlike most factory outlets, this outlet will sell over the phone and ship directly to your home. I have found the Martin family very pleasant and helpful over the years. If you are looking for outdoor furniture, please give them a call!

Vendor carries 1 manufacturer's lines

Darlee Outdoor Furniture

Decorators Choice ★★★

Furniture Avenue Galleries - 4350 Furniture Ave., Jamestown, NC, 27282

Hours: Monday-Saturday 9:30-6:00
Phone: 336-883-6104
Email: decoratorschoice@northstate.net
Website: None
Discount: 40%-50% off mfr retail
Payment: VISA, MasterCard, Personal Check
Delivery: White glove delivery

Decorator's Choice has some pretty good deals on special order furniture from a variety of lines, as well as on a small selection of showroom samples in new, first quality condition. Their styles run from traditional to transitional.

The store has recently opened clearance centers in one of the other Furniture Avenue Galleries showrooms and in the space that used to be occupied by Merones Italian restaurant.

Their quality is very good. They also have a good reputation for customer service. I've never heard a complaint about them from any reader, and they have a spotless record with the BBB.

If you're visiting High Point, you definitely should take time to visit the new showrooms in Jamestown, including Decorator's Choice.

Vendor carries 14 manufacturer's lines

Asiart	Harris Marcus	Trica
Collezione Europa	Magnussen Home	Vermont Precision
D. R. Kincaid	Morgan Stewart	Village Smith
Dinec	Null Furniture	Visions Elite
Greene Brothers	Pastel	

Distinctive Furnishings of Hickory ★★★★

Hickory Furniture Mart, U. S. Hwy. 70 SE, Hickory, NC, 28602

Hours: Monday-Saturday 9:00-6:00
Phone: 828-455-6062
Email: None
Website: www.distinctivefurnishingsofhickory.com
Discount: 40%-60% off mfr retail
Delivery: White glove delivery

Distinctive Furnishings of Hickory opened in early 2015 in the space formerly occupied by the National Home Furnishings Center on the first floor of the Hickory Furniture Mart. It is owned by the same company that has owned and operated the Heritage Furniture Outlet, Southern Style, and the Hooker Factory Outlet at the Hickory Furniture Mart for many years.

Although Distinctive Furnishings of Hickory is new, the parent company has a long history of excellent service. I have no hesitation about recommending them as a trusted resource.

E. J. Victor Factory Outlet

★★★★★

116 S. Lindsay St., High Point, NC, 27260

Hours: Monday-Friday 9:00-5:00, Saturday 10:00-3:00
Phone: 336-889-5500
Email: None
Website: None
Discount: 60%-75% off mfr retail
Payment: VISA, MasterCard, Personal Check
Delivery: White glove delivery

This is E. J. Victor's only factory outlet. This line is so high-end and exclusive that many people have never even heard of it. It's usually only carried by one or two very high-end stores in each state. They specialize in 18th and 19th century English reproductions. The furniture is very high-end, very high-quality, and frequently very ornate.

For what you get, however, the prices are actually quite good. As uptown as this furniture is, it won't break your bank account. Most pieces here are 55%-60% off retail.

On my most recent visit here, I found a great deal on a beautiful canopy bed from their "Julia Grey" collection (pictured on the following page). The bed retails for $11,756.00, but this floor sample I found at the outlet was priced at $5,195.00 -- 55% off retail! It was in perfect condition.

Like a few other High Point outlets, this showroom is closed during the months of April and October due to the High Point wholesale furniture markets. Sometimes, they remain closed a few days into May and November depending on how quickly they wrap up their work after the wholesale markets. Please call ahead to clarify the exact dates they will be closed before you visit.

The furniture here is gorgeous, and very high quality. These are pieces you will be able to give your grandchildren.

"Julia Grey" Canopy Bed from E. J. Victor

Retail: $11,756.00 Discounted price: $5,195.00
Savings at the E. J. Victor Factory Outlet: $6,561.00 = 55% off retail

Vendor carries 1 manufacturer's lines

E.J.Victor

Elite Designs ★★

Furniture Avenue Galleries, 4350 Furniture Ave., Jamestown, NC, 27282

Hours: Tuesday-Saturday 9:30-5:30
Phone: 336-885-1333
Email: None
Website: None
Discount: 30%-60% off mfr retail
Payment: Personal Check
Delivery: Nationwide white glove delivery

Elite Designs is owned by Kagan's Furniture. Ike Kagan also recently purchased the building that houses Furniture Avenue Galleries.

They have a nice selection of contemporary furniture at 30%-60% off retail. For example, on a recent visit I found this "Meti" bedroom set from Yuman Mod (pictured on the next page). The retail on this set, including the bed, two attached nightstands, dresser, 5 drawer tall chest, and mirror is $10,700.00, but you could buy this set off the floor for $7,135.00, a discount of $3,565.00 or 33% off retail.

The matching armoire retails for $2,396.00, but you could purchase the one in the showroom for 1,665.00, a discount of $731.00, or 31% off retail. All of the items in the showroom appeared to be in new, undamaged condition.

"Meti" bedroom set by Yuman Mod at Elite Designs

Retail: $13,096.00 Discounted price: $8,800.00
Savings at Elite Designs: $4,296.00 = 33% off retail

Vendor carries 9 manufacturer's lines

Aico (Michael Amini)	H Studio	Muniz Acrylic Furniture
Artmax	Johnston Casuals	Sharelle Furnishings
Elite Manufacturing	Lazar Industries	Yuman Mod

Ellenburg's Furniture

★★★★

I-40 & Stamey Farm Rd., Statesville, NC, 28687

Hours: Monday-Friday 8:30-5:30,
Saturday 9:30-4:30
Phone: 704-873-2900
Email: efurn@ellenburgs.com
Website: ellenburgs.com
Discount: 40%-60% off mfr retail
Payment: VISA, MasterCard, Personal
Check
Delivery: White glove delivery

Ellenburg's Furniture is located in Statesville, about 30 miles east of Hickory, NC, on I-40. They have a good selection of medium to high-end lines. They also have a small selection of closeout pieces and floor samples available at their showroom, as well as on their web site.

They carry all types of furniture, but they specialize in wicker and rattan. If you're looking for high end indoor or outdoor wicker and rattan, this is a very knowledgable source.

Ellenburg's has an excellent reputation for service. Their BBB record has been spotless for years, and I've never heard a single complaint about them.

If you're in the Statesville area, you may wish to stop in. If you're looking for special order furniture from any of the lines below, you definitely should call Ellenburg's and ask them to quote a price.

Vendor carries 62 manufacturer's lines

Acacia Furniture	Bob Timberlake	Chelsea House
American Drew	Braxton Culler	Classic Georgian
American Heritage	Breezesta	Classic Rattan
AP Generations	Capel Rugs	Designer Wicker & Rattan
Bassett	Capris Furniture	Drexel Heritage
Beachcraft Mfg.	Castelle	Ebel
Beachfront Furniture	Century Furniture	Erwin & Sons
Bernhardt	Charleston Forge	Ficks Reed

Harden	Lloyd/Flanders	Shady Lady Lighting
Hekman	Lo Brothers	South Sea Rattan
Henredon	Lyon Shaw	Stein World
Henry Link	Maitland-Smith	Tradewinds
Highland House	New River Artisans	Uwharrie Chair
Jonathan Charles	Padma's Plantation	Venture By Lane
Kingsley-Bate	Polywood	Wellington Hall
KNF Designs	Pride	Whitecraft Rattan
Lane	Pulaski	Wildwood Lamps
Laneventure	Regency House	Woodard Furniture
Lea Industries	Sarreid	Woodmark Furniture
Legacy Classic	Seaside Casual Furniture	Yesteryear Wicker
Lexington	Sedgefield By Adams	

European Furniture Importers ★★★

2145 W. Grand Ave., Chicago, IL, 60612

Hours: Monday-Friday 10:00-7:00,
Saturday 10:00-6:00, Sunday12:00-5:00
Phone: 312-243-1955 / 800-283-1955
Email: richard@eurofurniture.com
Website: eurofurniture.com
Discount: 20%-60% off mfr retail
Payment: VISA, MasterCard, Discover,
Personal Check
Delivery: White glove delivery

European Furniture Importers has greatly improved their customer service since the last edition of this book. They now have an A+ rating with the BBB, with only one resolved complaint within the last three years, as of this writing in March 2016.

They have an extensive inventory of modern and contemporary furniture. Definitely compare their prices at their order number above if you are considering ordering furniture from any of the brands below.

Vendor carries 39 manufacturer's lines

Alutec Furniture	Copeland Furniture	Lafer
American Leather	Dellarobbia	Luxy Furniture
Au Furniture	DomItalia Furniture	Magis Design Furniture
BDI/Becker Designed	Ekornes	Midj Furniture
Blu Dot Furniture	Elite Leather	Origlia Furniture
Bontempi	Elite Manufacturing	Pedrali Furniture
Calligaris	Focus One Home	Porada Furniture
Casamania Furniture	Gamma Arredamenti	PSM Italy Furniture
Casprini Furniture	Geneva Lab	Roland Simmons Co
Castagnetti Furniture	Huppe	Sicea Furniture
Cattelan Italia Furniture	Kartell Furniture	Sitland Furniture
Ciacci Kreaty Furniture	Kristalia Furniture	Softline Furniture
Colico Furniture	La Palma Furniture	Vittorio Marchetti

Far Eastern Furnishings ★★★★

Hickory Furniture Mart - U. S. Hwy 70 SE, Level 3, Hickory, NC, 28602

Hours: Monday-Saturday 9:00-6:00
Phone: 828-256-9500
Email: stanley@fareasternfurnishings.com
Website: fareasternfurnishings.com
Discount: Factory direct pricing to public
Payment: VISA, MasterCard, American Express, Discover, Personal Check
Delivery: They only ship to the eastern half of the U. S., east of the Mississippi River. Please call for shipping details

Far Eastern Furnishings at the Hickory Furniture Mart is owned by FEFCO, a company that has been manufacturing high end furniture in Asia and importing it to North America for over 65 years. They are factory direct to the public.

Their product line consists of casegoods for the bedroom, dining room, and living room in traditional Asian designs. The quality is good. All pieces are made of solid rosewood, ebony, or teak. Some pieces are intricately carved.

It is difficult to determine how their deals compare to other sources. Their products are very unique, and they sell only to the public at a set price. Overall, I would say they offer good value for money.

As an example, on my most recent visit I saw a lovely carved 60" round dining room table with eight chairs for only $4,500, pictured on the next page. That is a good deal for this level of quality.

They also have a beautiful collection of jade accessories, including a jade tower valued at over $280,000.00.

If you're looking for unique furniture with a strong Asian look, this is a good source to contact. They have a spotless record with the BBB, and I've never received any complaints about them. They do offer the usual decorator discounts and a military discount, so if you are in any of the armed services, be sure to ask for special pricing.

Dining Room Set from Far Eastern Furnishings

Importer price direct to public: $4,500.00

Vendor carries 1 manufacturer's lines

FEFCO

Fran's Wicker & Rattan Furniture ★★★

295 Route 10 East, Succasunna, NJ, 07876

Hours: Monday-Wednesday 9:00-5:30, Thursday-Friday 9:00-8:30, Saturday 9:00-6:00, Sunday 12:00-5:00
Phone: 973-584-2230 / 800-372-6799
Email: sales@franswicker.com
Website: franswicker.com
Discount: 50% off mfr retail
Payment: VISA, MasterCard, American Express, Discover, Personal Check
Delivery: Curbside delivery only

Fran's Wicker & Rattan has been discounting wicker for over 35 years. Most of their furniture and accessories are made in their own factories in China, Indonesia, and the Philippines. They have a huge catalog. They also have an enormous showroom just to the west of Newark -- over 100,000 square feet.

Fran's can also order many other brands of wicker and rattan at significant discounts. They will not give out a list of the specific brands they have access to, but they will give you a comparison price over the phone if you call with a specific brand and item number. I have found that they can order most national brands.

They also have a clearance center, which has a nice selection of discontinued styles and floor samples at up to 60% off retail. You can see their clearance items online at their Web site.

Fran's Wicker and Rattan has greatly improved their customer service. They now have an A+ rating with the BBB, as of this writing in February 2016.

Furniture Avenue Galleries

★★

4250 Furniture Avenue, Jamestown, NC, 27282

Hours: Monday-Saturday 9:30-5:30
Phone: None
Email: None
Website: None

Furniture Avenue Galleries in Jamestown, NC, opened in early summer 2005. Recently, they have lost a number of important tenants. Robert Bergelin, King's Chandelier, and Hinkle Furniture have all closed. Far Eastern Furnishings and Leather & More have moved to the Hickory Furniture Mart. Merones Italian Restaurant has also closed.

Only three companies remain here: American Accents, Kagan's Furniture, and Decorator's Choice. Please see these individual listings for further details on each store. Please note that Savi Home Furnishings and Elite Designs are actually a part of Kagan's Furniture. Savi Home Furnishings specializes in home office furniture, and Elite Designs has contemporary styles.

Please also note that Furniture Avenue no longer has extended hours on Thursday and Friday evenings. The new hours are posted above.

There are some good deals to be found here if you are in the High Point area, especially on clearance items. Jamestown is less than 10 minutes drive from downtown High Point.

Furniture Outlet of Ridgeway ★★★★

6812 Greensboro Rd., Ridgeway, VA, 24148

Hours: Monday-Saturday 9:00-6:00, Sunday 1:00-5:00
Phone: 276-956-2699
Email: See store web site
Website: furnitureoutletofridgeway.com
Discount: 50%-75% off mfr retail
Payment: VISA, MasterCard, American Express, Discover
Delivery: White glove delivery

Furniture Outlet of Ridgeway is a great resource. Most of their stock is outlet furniture from Pulaski. Since Pulaski closed their only factory outlet in October 2008, this is now the primary source for Pulaski seconds, discontinued items, and showroom samples.

There are some great deals here. All of the Pulaski case goods I saw were at least 50% off retail, and many as much as 75% off. Many items were in new condition. A few had small flaws, such as a tiny scratch.

They also have good deals on Ridgeway clocks and furniture from Stein World, as well as some very nice imported pieces. Recently, they have added closeout pieces from Ashley and Hooker.

This store has a spotless record with the BBB. I am impressed with the staff, and with the references from nearby furniture industry professionals with whom I've worked for years. I highly recommend this store as a resource.

Vendor carries 5 manufacturer's lines

Ashley Furniture	Pulaski	Stein World
Hooker	Ridgeway Clocks	

Furnitureland On Main

2200 S. Main St., High Point, NC, 27263

Hours: Monday 8:00-7:00,
Thursday-Saturday 8:00-7:00
Phone: 336-841-8599
Email: sales@furniturelandsouth.com
Website: None
Discount: 50%-75% off mfr retail
Payment: VISA, MasterCard, Personal
Check
Delivery: White glove delivery

Furnitureland On Main occupies the same 40,000 square foot showroom that used to be occupied by Furnitureland Salvage. Now, instead of housing Furnitureland South's quick ship program, this space liquidates returned merchandise, floor samples, and overstock pieces.

The clearance items here in the main building are mostly in new first quality condition. There are some complete sets and some incomplete sets. Please see the listing for *Furnitureland South* for a complete listing of the manufacturers whose products you may find here.

The second building in the back is marked "Accessories and Art", but it actually contains mostly furniture as well. Please note that almost all of the items back here have some sort of damage, but many are still good deals if you are willing to spend time fixing up a piece or replacing missing hardware. Here you will also find lamps, chandeliers, vases, clocks, mirrors, desks, and odd chairs.

Furnitureland South

★★★★

5635 Riverdale Dr., Jamestown, NC, 27282

Hours: Monday-Thursday 8:30-5:30,
Friday 8:30-8:30, Saturday 8:30-5:30
Phone: 336-841-4328 / 866-436-8056
Email: sales@furniturelandsouth.com
Website: furniturelandsouth.com
Discount: 40%-60% off mfr retail
Payment: Personal Check
Delivery: In home with full setup

Furnitureland South is one of the biggest telephone discounters of furniture in North Carolina. If you want to see a huge selection of furniture all in one place, this is a great place to visit.

Most of the new special order furniture at the main Furnitureland South store is offered at about 40%-50% off retail, with a wide selection of clearance items offered at about 60%-65% off retail. Most new accessories run about 25% off retail. Discounts on new furniture may vary throughout the year due to limited time promotions.

For example, on my most recent visit I found this floor sample dining room set from Marge Carson offered at about 63% off retail (pictured on the following page). It was in new condition with no flaws I could see, which is typical for Furnitureland South clearance items from the main showrooms.

The manufacturer's retail price on this set was $63,238.00. This includes eight side chairs, two arm chairs, the dining table, and two bunching display cabinets.

Furnitureland South's price to purchase this one floor sample set off the showroom floor was $24,631.00, or about 63% off the manufacturer's retail. The customer must purchase the entire floor sample set to receive the clearance price. None of the pieces were offered individually. This is the best pricing I've seen in North Carolina on Marge Carson furniture.

Furnitureland South offers additional discounts to employees of large corporations, such as IBM and UPS. Please see their most current list of companies which receive extra discounts at their web site.

You will find a wide variety of clearance furniture throughout the showroom at similar discounts. To find even greater discounts on furniture, head across the back parking lot to Furnitureland South's Clearance Center.

The Furnitureland South Cafe is a good stop for lunch. There is a Starbucks just inside the entrance of the main Mart building with free wireless connectivity, a free "man cave" with a big screen tv to occupy bored husbands and children, and a free shuttle bus to selected area hotels.

Furnitureland South's customer service has greatly improved over past years. They now have an A+ rating with the BBB. If you visit in person and find your furniture among their clearance items, you will get a very good deal on furniture in excellent condition. If you call this source to special order furniture to be delivered at a later date, you will find excellent discounts on many of the brands they carry.

Marge Carson dining room set at Furnitureland South

Retail: $63,238.00 Discounted price: $24,631.00
Savings at Furnitureland South: $38,607.00 = 63% off retail

Vendor carries 904 manufacturer's lines

2 Day Designs
828 Intl Trading
A La Carte
A R T Furniture
A. A. Laun
A. J. Floyd
A.P. Generations
Abigails
Acacia Furniture
Accent Decor
Accessories Abroad
Acme Metal Products
Action by Lane
Adventure Marketing
Affordable Designs/Lloyds
African Market
Agio International
Aico (Michael Amini)
Ainsley Lamp
Alan White
Alfresco Home
Alivar by Leif Petersen
All Continental
Allan Copley
Allen Anderson
Allen McDaniel
Allusions
Alpharville Design
Althorp Living History
Amanda Sutton
Ambella Home
Ambiance Lighting
American Bedding
American Drew
American Mirror

Amity Imports
Ancient Mosaic Studios
Anderson & Daishi
Andrew Pearson Design
Anglo Oriental
Anichini
Ann Gish
Anthology
Antler Art
AP Generations
ARC/COM
Architex Intl Fabrics
Ardley Hall
Art & Frame Direct
Art Classics, Ltd.
Art d'Elite
Art Evolution
Art Image
Art Up
Artagraph
Artanica
Arte de Mexico
Arte Italica
Arteriors Imports
Artisan House, inc
Artisan's Design Guild
Artistica Metal Designs
Artists Guild of America
Artitalia Group
Artland
Artmasters Collection
Artmax
Asay Import Export
Ashley Manor
Aspen Furniture

Atlanta Glasscrafters
Aubergine Home
Austin Sculpture
Austin's Farm Ent
Austin-Gray
Authentic Models
Avantglide
Azzolin Bros. Importers
B & K Components Ltd
Baldwin Hardware
Banana Fish
Barbara Barry
Barbara Cosgrove Lamps
Barcalounger
Bassett Mirror
Basta Sole by Tropitone
Bauer International
Bausman
Beachcraft Mfg.
Bedding Inspirations
Bedford Cottage
Bedtime
Bella Rose
Belle Epoque
Bellino Fine Linens
Benchcraft
Benicia Foundry
Benjamin Rugs
Bentley Churchill
Berco Tableworks
Berg Furniture
Berkline
Bermex International
Bernhardt
Berry Creek Home

Best Chair
Bestar
Better Homes
Bevan-Funnell
Bibi
Big Fish Art
Bluefish Home
Bob Timberlake
Bodrum Group
Bolier
Bontempi
Bougainvillea
Boussac Fadini
Bradburn Galleries
Bradington Young
Bramble Company
Braxton Culler
Brent Jacobs
Brimar
Brookwood
Broughton Hall
Brown Jordan
Broyhill
Brushstrokes
Bulova
Bush Furniture
Butler Electric
Butler Specialty
C. R. Laine Upholstery
Caffco International
Cal-Bear
Cal-Style
Calcot Ltd
California House
California Kids Bedding
Canal Dover
Candella Lighting
Canvas Company
Cape Craftsmen
Capris Furniture

Caracole
Carey Moore Designs
Carolina Mirror
Carpet Creation
Carter Furniture
Casa Fiora
Casa Novalia
Casana
Casey Collection
Cast Classics
Cast Craft
Castelle
Central Oriental
Century Furniture
CFI Manufacturing
Chandler Collection
Chapman Lamps
Charles Alan
Chatham Crossing
Chelsea Frank Group
Chelsea House
Chicago Textiles
Child Craft
Chipper & Bailey
Christopher Guy
Christy USA
Chromcraft
Clark Casual
Classic Cushions
Classic Elements
Classic Flame
Classic Gallery
Classic Leather
Classic Rattan
Clayton & Company
Clayton Marcus
Clearwater American
Cloud Nine Comforts
CMI - Colonial Mills
Coast To Coast Leather

Cochrane Furniture
Cocoons
Collections 85
Colonial Furniture
Color Shop
Columbine Cody
Comfor-Pedic
Comfort Research
Comfortaire
Company C
Compositions By Schnadig
Con-Tab
Conover Chair
Conrad Grebel
Containers 2 Go
Corsican Furniture
Councill
Country Originals
Cox Manufacturing Co
Craft-Tex
Craftique
Craftwork Guild
Cramer
Creations At Dallas
Creative Accents
Creative Decor
Creative Elegance
Creative Fine Arts
Creative Images
Creative Sign Language
Cross Plains Imports
Crystal Clear Industries
CTH Sherrill Occasional
Currey & Co.
Curvet USA
CWL Designs
D & F Wicker Rattan
D. B. Sources
D. B. South
D. K. Living

Dale Tiffany
Dalyn Rug Company
Danao Outdoor
Dash & Albert
Davenport
Davis & Davis Rugs
Davis International
Davis Office Furniture
Dayva International
Decorative Arts
Decorative Crafts
Defehr Furniture
Deitz and Sons
Delos Inc.
Design Guild
Design Source
Design Systems
Designs By Robert Guenther
Designtex
Dimplex
Directional
Distinction Leather
Distinctive Designs
Distinctive Oils
DLH Garden
DMI Custom Bedspreads
DMI Furniture
Downtown Company
Dream Weavers
Dreamfit
Dura Hold
Duralee Fabrics
Dutailier
DWI Holdings
E.J.Victor
East End Imports
Eastern Accents
Eastern Legends
Eckadams/Vogel Peterson
Eddy West

Edelman Leather
Ekornes
Elaine Smith Pillows
Elden Collections
Elements By Grapevine
Elisabeth Marshall
Elite Leather
Elite Manufacturing
Elliotts Designs
Ello
Elysee Collection
Emdee International
Emerson et Cie
Emerson Smith
Emess Design Group
Emissary Trading
Encore
Endura Furniture

Englander Bedding
ESI Ergonomic Solutions
Espino
European Home Designs
Eurostyle
Evan Du Four
Evans Ceramics
Evans Frame Shop
Excelsior
Excelsior-Nicole Miller
Expressive Designs Rugs
Fabric To Frame
Fabrica International
Fairfield Chair
Farmhouse/Oliver Walker
Fashion Bed Group
Ferguson Copeland
FFDM
Ficks Reed
Fine Art Lamps
Fine Art Ltd.
Fixtures Furniture

Flair Design
Flair International
Flambro Imports
Flexsteel
Floober Brothers
Florida Blinds & Drapery
Florita Nova
Focus Rugs
Foreside Company
Forma Design
Foster's Point
Four Hands
Four Seasons
Fourbro Frames
Francesco Molon
Freckles
Frederick Cooper
Fremarc Designs

French Broad River Decoy
French Heritage
Friedman Brothers
Furniture Designs/Choice
Fusion Designs
Fusion Z
G. A. Brinkel
Gallery
Garrett Leather
Garrett Mirror Support
George Kovacs Lighting
Georgian Furnishings
Gianni
Giorgio Collection
Glass Arts
Global Views, Inc.
Gloster
Go Home
Gotico
Grand Rapids Chair
Grange
Great Impressions

Great River Trading	Hollywoods	Jaunty Company
Green Frog Art	Holton Galleries	Jaynor Furnishings
Greenhouse Design	Home Fires	Jeffco
Griffin Creek	Home Treasures	Jenkins Lamp & Shade
Guardsman	Hooker	Jensen Jarrah Leisure
Guildmaster	Howard Elliott Collection	Jeremie Corp
Gunlocke	Howard Miller	Jessica Charles
Guy Chaddock	Hubbardton Forge	JLF
H. Bridges	Hugh Moffitt	John Boos & Co.
H. K. H. Intl	Human Touch	John Charles Designs
H. Potter	Humane Trophies	John Matouk & Co
Habersham	Huntington Furniture	John-Richard
Halcyon	Huntington House	Johnston Casuals
Hallmart Collectibles	Huppe	Jon Elliott Upholstery
Hamilton Collections	Hurtado	Jonathan Charles
Hammary	Hyundai Furniture	Jordan-Alexander
Hancock & Moore	Idea Industries	Joya Sleep Systems
Harco Loor	Ideal Originals	JSF Industries
Harden	Import Collection	JSP-LES Industries
Harris Marcus	Inmon Enterprises	Jubilee
Harrison Import & Export	Inner Asia	Julia Gray
Hart Associates	Integra	Just Accents
Havaseat	Interlude	Justin Camlin
HBF	International Arts	K & K Interiors
Hedge Row Outdoors	Intl Contemporary Design	Kalco
Heirloom	Intrada	Karastan
Hekman	Iron Beds of America	Karges
Hellenic Rugs	Isenhour Furniture	Katha Diddel Home
Hemsley	Italsofa	Kathy Ireland
Hen-Feathers	J. B. Watts	Kaven Company
Henredon	J. D. Chamberlain	Kaymed
Henry Link	J. D. Store Equipment	Keleen Leathers
Hickory Heritage	J. H. Craver & Son	Kennebunk Home
Hickory Springs	Jaipur Rugs	Kenroy International
Hickory White	James R. Cooper	Kessler
High Point Furniture	Jamie Young Lamps	Key City Furniture
High Smith Furniture	Jan Barboglio	Kichler Lighting
Highland House	Jason Scott Collection	Kidcraft
Historic Golf Prints	Jasper Cabinet	Kincaid
Holga	Jasper Seating Co.	Kinder-Harris

King Hickory
King Koil
Kingsley Manor
Kingsley-Bate
KNF Designs
Knickerbocker Bed
Koch & Lowy
Koch Originals
Koko Company
Kravet Fabrics
Krug
La Barge
Ladybug
Ladyslipper
Lakol Inc.
Lam Lee
Lambs & Ivy
Lamp Works
Lane
Laneventure
Largo
Latex Foam Products
Lauren Brooks
Laurent Leather
Laurie Bell, LLC
Laurier Furniture
Lazar Industries
Le Blanc Linen Wash
Lea Industries
Leatherbound Antiques
Leathercraft
Leathermart
LeatherTrend
Lee Kennedy
Lee Wilder Bedwear
Leeazanne
Leedo Furniture
Legacy Classic
Legacy Home
Legendary Art

Leggett and Platt
Leisters Furniture
Leisure House
Lenox Lighting
Lexington
Liberty
Ligna
Lillian August
Limonta Home
Linrene Furniture
Linwood
Lite Source Inc.
Lloyd/Flanders
Lodi Down & Feather
Loft 102 For the Home
Lorts
Lotfy & Sons
Lt. Moses Willard
Lucia Cassa Textiles
Lux-Art Silks
Lyon Shaw
M. T. S. Besana-Carrara
Magna Design
Magnussen Home
Maharam
Maitland-Smith
Majestic Mirror
Mallin
Manchester Furniture
Mansour Rahmanan & Co
Mantua Manufacturing
Marcella Fine Rugs
Mardan Publishing
Marge Carson
Mario & Marielena
Mark David
Mark Roberts
Marquis CLL
Marquis CSTM Contract
Martha Stewart

Marvel
Mary Mayo Designs
Masland Carpet & Rugs
Mason Maloof
Mass Imports
Mastercraft
Masterlooms Rugs
Masterpiece Accessories
Mathews and Company
Matrix
Mayer Fabrics
Mayline
McKay Table Pads
McNeilly Champion
Meadowcraft
MER Rugs
Metropolitan Galleries
Mikhail Darafeev
Miles Talbott
Millender
Miller Desk
Minoff Lamps
Mirador
Mirror Craft
Mohawk
Momeni
Momentum Textiles
Montaage
Montage
Moore and Giles
Motioncraft
Movi
MTS
Murray Feiss Lighting
MWB Designs
Mystic Valley Traders
N. C. Souther
Nan Wood Hall Fine Art
Naos
Napa Home and Garden

Napsax by Artisan's Guild	Palmyra	Profile Lighting & Design
Natale Furniture Industries	PAMA	Progressive Furniture
Natural Light	Paper White	Propac Images
Nature's Gallery	Paragon Picture	Protect-A-Bed
Natures Rest Marketing	Park Avenue Lamps	Pulaski
Natuzzi	Parker Southern	PUR Cashmere
Nautica Home	Pastel	Pure Touch/Therapedic
NDI	Pastiche	Quality Cushion Factory
NE Kids	Pavilion	Quoizel
Nelson Garfield	Payne Street Imports	R. C. Furniture
Neutral Posture	Pearson	R. Rogers Designs
New Century Picture	Peel & Company	Rachlin
New River Artisans	Pennsylvania House	Raffia
Nirvana Swing Co.	Perfect Touch	Ragon House Collection
Noonoo Rug Company	Peter Fasano	Ralph Lauren
North Bay Collections	Peters-Revington	Rare Collections-San Segal
Northern Fine Arts	Phoenix Galleries	Raschella Collection
Nuance Fine Furniture	Piage & Pieta	Ready-To-Bed
Null Furniture	Picture Galleries	Regency House
O. D. E. Fine Art	Picture It	Regina Andrew Design
O. L. F.	Picture Source	Reliable Bedding
O. W. Lee	Pictures Plus	Reliance Lamp Co
Oklahoma Importing	Pieri Creations	Rembrandt Lamps
Old Hickory Furniture	Pindler & Pindler	Remington Lamp
Old Java	Pine Cone Hill	Ren-Wil
Old World Stone & Iron	Pine Creek Bedding	Replica
OLF Lamps	Platt Collections	Restonic
Olympia	Plenty's Horn	Reverie Dreamy Linens
Oopsy Daisy	Pointe of View	Richardson Bros
Opus Designs	Pollack Fabrics	Ridgeway Clocks
Orbit	Polo Ralph Lauren	Riverside Furniture
Oriental Weavers	Pompeii	Riverwood
Orleans	Portobello Intl	Riztex USA - Hometex Co.
Osborne & Little	Potluck Studios	Robert Abbey Lamps
Oscar de la Renta	Powell	Robert Allen Fabrics
P & P Chair	Precedent	Robert Bergelin
Pacific Coast Lighting	Premier Furniture	Robin Bruce
Padma's Plantation	Presidential Billiards	Rockwood
Palecek	Pride	Romweber
Palliser	Privilege Fine Furniture	Rowe Furniture

Rug Barn
Ryan Studio
Sagefield Leather
Salem Graphics
Saloom
Sam Moore
Samsonite
Sandicast
Sarreid
Sarut Group
Savoir Faire
Savoy House
Scalamandre Fabrics
Schnadig
Schumacher Fabrics
Scott Thomas
Screen Gems
SDH Linens
Sea Gull Lighting
Seabrook Wallcovering
Seahawk Designs
Sealy
Sean Fox Design
Seco Furniture
Second Avenue
Second Impressions
Sedgefield By Adams
Selva Style
Serta
Seven Seas Seating
Sferra Brothers
Shadow Catchers
Shadow Mountain
Shady Lady Lighting
Sharelle Furnishings
Shashi Cann
Shaw Flooring
Shelby Williams
Sherrill
Sierrarts

Signature Fabrics
Signature Rugs
Silk-Like
Simmons
Sina Pearson Textiles
Sleep Fusion
Sligh
Slip
SofaTrend
Soft Idea & Apparel
Somerset
Sonneman
South Cone Trading Co.
Southeastern Kids
Southern Textiles
Southport Furniture
Southwood
Spring Air
St. Timothy
Stacy Garcia
Stanford
Stanley
Star Embroidery
Statesville Chair
Stein World
Sterling Industries
Steve Silver Furniture
Steven Drew Int'l
Stock Market
Stone County Ironworks
Stone International
Stonegate Designs
Stoneleigh
Story & Clark Pianos
Storytime
Stratford
Stray Dog
Strobel Technologies
Stroheim & Romann
Style Upholstering

Stylecraft Lamps
Stylelife Furniture
Stylex
Sumter Cabinet
Superior Furniture
Supreme Mattress
Sustainable Lifestyles
Swaim
T. S. Berry
Table Designs
Tag Furnishings Group
Tapestries Ltd.
Taracea Custom
Taracea USA
Taylor King
Telescope
Temple
Tempur-pedic
Textillery
Thayer Coggin
The Import Collection
Theodore Alexander
Thief River Linens
Thred Pillows
Three Coins
Timmerman
Tinnin Oriental Carpets
Tomasini Fine Linens
Tommy Bahama
Top Brass
Topstar
Touchstone Fine Art
Toyo Trading Company
Tozai Home
Trade Associate Group
Trade Associates Group
Tradewinds by LaneVenture
Trans-Ocean Import Co
Treasure Garden
Tree Factory

Tree Masters
Trees Etc.
Trees International
Trend Lighting
Trevor James
Trica
Triune
Tropitone
Trowbridge Gallery
Two Day Designs
Two Oceans Art & Design
Two's Company
Tyndall Creek
Tyne House of Lewes
Ultegra
Ultimate Accents
Ultrasuede by Toray
Unique Originals
Universal Floor Display
Universal Furniture
University Loft Company
USA Premium Leather
Uttermost
Uwharrie Chair
Valley Forge Fabrics
Valspar
Van Teal

Vanguard Furniture
Vanguard Pictures
Vasco International
Vaughan Bassett
Vaughan Furniture
Veneman
Venetian Gems
Venture By Lane
Vermont Tubbs
Versailles Fine Linens
Versteel
Victorian Classics
Villency Contract
Vinings Imports
Vintage
Vintage Verandah
Visual Comfort
Vitafoam Feather Beds
Vitalie
Vogel Peterson
Wara Tapestries
Watson Furniture
Weiman
Wesley Allen
Wesley Hall
West Brothers
Westwood Interiors

Westwood Lamps
What a Clever Girl
Whitecraft Rattan
Whittemore-Sherrill
Wildcat Territory
Wildwood Lamps
William H. Williams
Willow Creek
Windsor Home
Wingard
Winston
Woodard Furniture
Woodard Landgrave
Woodmark Furniture
Worlds Away
Woven Art Studio
Woven Workz
Wynwood
Yorkshire House
Young America by Stanley
Young Hinkle
ZedBed
Zodax
Zoom Seating
Zrike

Good's Home Furnishings ★★★★

Hickory Furniture Mart - U. S. Hwy 70 SE, Level 2 & 3, Hickory, NC, 28602

Hours: Monday-Saturday 9:00-6:00
Phone: 828-855-3220
Email: info@goodshomefurnishings.com
Website: goodshomefurnishings.com
Discount: 35%-70% off mfr retail
Payment: VISA, MasterCard, American Express, Discover, Personal Check
Delivery: White glove delivery

Good's Home Furnishings is a great source for a wide variety of special order furniture brands at 40%-50% off retail. They also have a great selection of clearance items in new, first-quality condition on the sales floor at 60%-75% off retail.

For example, on a recent visit I found a great deal on a beautiful high-quality "Galoway" bookcase from Ralph Lauren Furniture, pictured at left. The manufacturer's retail on this piece is $11,385.00, but you could special order this item new from Good's Home Furnishings for only $6,499.00. That's a savings of 43% off retail!

The BBB gives this store an A rating as of this writing in February 2016, with 13 resolved complaints within the last year. The BBB notes that their rating of this store was lowered due to the [short] "length of time the business has been operating".

Consumers should know that this really isn't comparable to a new business due to the co-owners' long history in the furniture industry while they were both principals at Boyles Furniture. I worked with Randy Good (co-owner of Good's Home Furnishings) for many years at Boyles, and I have always been pleased with the way he helped my private clients and tour groups. In my experience, Good's Home Furnishings is a very reputable source.

If you are interested in any of the brands listed below, you should call Good's for a comparison quote. If you are shopping in person in North Carolina, you should definitely check out their showroom at the Hickory Furniture Mart for great deals on floor samples and other clearance items.

Ralph Lauren "Galoway" bookcase at Good's Home Furnishings

Retail: $11,385.00 Discounted price: $6,499.00
Savings at Good's Home Furnishings: $4886.00 = 43% off retail

---

Vendor carries 41 manufacturer's lines

Alfresco Home
Baker Furniture
Bernhardt
Better Homes
Bradington Young
Butler Specialty
CMI - Colonial Mills
Conrad Grebel
CTH Sherrill Occasional
Drexel Heritage
Fashion Bed Group
Ferguson Copeland
Four Hands
Guy Chaddock

Henkel Harris
Henredon
Hooker
John-Richard
Lexington
Linwood
Motioncraft
Paula Deen Home
Pennsylvania House
Precedent
Sam Moore
Seven Seas Seating
Sherrill
Sligh

Southwood
Stanley
Taylor King
Theodore Alexander
Thomasville
Tommy Bahama
Trump Home
Turning House Furniture
Universal Furniture
Vanguard Furniture
Whittemore-Sherrill
Windham Castings
Young America by Stanley

Green Front Furniture (Farmville) ★★★★

316 N. Main St., Farmville, VA, 23901

Hours: Monday-Friday 10:00-5:30, Saturday 9:00-6:00
Phone: 434-392-5943
Email: greenfrontva@greenfront.com
Website: greenfront.com
Discount: 40%-50% off mfr retail
Payment: VISA, MasterCard, Discover, Personal Check
Delivery: White glove delivery

Green Front Furniture's main store and telephone sales operation is located in Farmville, VA, just west of Richmond. The store complex is huge, covering 4 city blocks. There are large galleries for Henredon, Sherrill, and Henkel Harris. They also carry many other medium to high-end lines of furniture and accessories.

The discounts on brand new first-quality furniture, whether bought in person or over the phone, run from 40%-50% off retail. There is also a clearance center on site (The Boneyard) which has even better deals.

This location has an excellent reputation for customer service. As of this writing in February 2016, they have an A+ rating with the BBB with no complaints in the last three years.

If you are near Farmville, VA, it's worth making a stop at their clearance center - "The Boneyard". They have some great deals on furniture, rugs, lamps, and accessories.

Vendor carries 135 manufacturer's lines

A & B	Artistica Metal Designs	Carver's Guild
A.P. Industries	Asian Imports	Century Furniture
Allstate	Austin Productions	Chinese Imports
Althorp Living History	Barcalounger	Colonial Furniture
Art Gallery	Bayne	Columbia
Art In Motion	Big Fish Art	Congoleum
Arthur Court	Bradington Young	Cooper Classics

Craftmaster Furniture
CTH Sherrill Occasional
Currey & Co.
Custom Shoppe
David Michael
Denny Lamps
Down Right
Duckworth Fine Arts
Durham Furniture
E.J.Victor
Eastern Accents
Elite Manufacturing
Epic Leather
Fanimation
Ferguson Copeland
FFDM
Formica
Four Seasons
Frederick Cooper
Friedman Brothers
GKI
Global Views, Inc.
Habersham
Hanamint
Hancock & Moore
Harden
Hekman
Henkel Harris
Henredon
Henry Link
Hickory Chair
Highland House
Home Source
Hooker
Howard Miller
Huntington House
Interlude
Jason Scott Collection

Jessica Charles
John-Richard
Jonathan Charles
K & K Interiors
Karndean Tile
KAS
King Hickory
Kingsley-Bate
Lane
Laneventure
Leathercraft
Legacy Leather
Leisters Furniture
Lexington
Lloyd/Flanders
Loloi Rugs
Maitland-Smith
Majestic Mirror
Mark Roberts
Marshall James
Meadowcraft
Michael Thomas
Miles Talbott
Mobel
Mohawk
Motioncraft
Murray Feiss Lighting
Mystic Valley Traders
NDI
Olympia
Palatial Leather
Paragon Picture
Paul Robert
Pawley's Island
Pergo
Pinehurst Umbrellas
Possible Dreams
Precedent

Quoizel
Ragno Porcelain
Ralph Lauren
Randall-Allan
Regency Leather
Saloom
Sedgefield By Adams
Serta
Seven Seas Seating
Shadow Catchers
Shaw Flooring
Sherrill
Sligh
Southhampton
Southwood
Spanish Imports
Stanford
Sweet Dreams Linens
Taracea
Taylor King
Theodore Alexander
Timeworks
Toepperwein's
Tommy Bahama
Tradewinds
Treasure Garden
Tropitone
Tyndale
Uttermost
Uwharrie Chair
Venture By Lane
Wesley Allen
West Brothers
Whittemore-Sherrill
Wildwood Lamps
Winners Only
Woodard Furniture
Zimmerman

Green Front Furniture (Manassas) ★★★

10154 Harry J. Parrish Blvd, Manassas, VA, 20109

Hours: Monday-Saturday 10:00-6:00, Sunday12:00-5:00
Phone: 703-396-8560
Email: sales@greenfront.com
Website: greenfront.com
Discount: 40%-50% off mfr retail
Payment: VISA, MasterCard, Discover, Personal Check
Delivery: White glove delivery

Green Front Furniture's Northern Virginia location has moved to Manassas, VA from Sterling, VA. They have a very nice selection of medium to high-end lines, including Lexington, Hooker, Sherrill, and Maitland-Smith.

All of Green Front's floor samples and discontinued styles from their three stores and their phone sales service are all sent to their clearance center at their other location in Farmville, VA. For this reason, there is no monetary advantage to shopping at this location in person. All the furniture here is new, and you get the same price whether you buy in person or over the phone.

If you are near Farmville, VA, it's worth making a stop at their clearance center - "The Boneyard". They have some great deals on furniture, rugs, lamps, and accessories. Otherwise, most people would be better off saving the drive and just ordering from this source over the phone.

Green Front's Manassas location has a spotless record with the BBB. They're definitely a good source to check out.

Vendor carries 132 manufacturer's lines

A & B	Artistica Metal Designs	Bradington Young
Allstate	Asian Imports	Carver's Guild
Althorp Living History	Austin Productions	Century Furniture
Art Gallery	Barcalounger	Chinese Imports
Art In Motion	Bayne	Colonial Furniture
Arthur Court	Big Fish Art	Columbia

Congoleum
Cooper Classics
Craftmaster Furniture
CTH Sherrill Occasional
Currey & Co.
Custom Shoppe
David Michael
Denny Lamps
Down Right
Duckworth Fine Arts
Durham Furniture
E.J.Victor
Eastern Accents
Elite Manufacturing
Epic Leather
Fanimation
Ferguson Copeland
FFDM
Formica
Four Seasons
Frederick Cooper
Friedman Brothers
GKI
Global Views, Inc.
Habersham
Hanamint
Hancock & Moore
Harden
Hekman
Henkel Harris
Henredon
Henry Link
Hickory Chair
Highland House
Home Source
Hooker
Howard Miller
Huntington House

Interlude
Jason Scott Collection
Jessica Charles
John-Richard
Jonathan Charles
K & K Interiors
Karndean Tile
KAS
King Hickory
Kingsley-Bate
Lane
Laneventure
Leathercraft
Legacy Leather
Leisters Furniture
Lexington
Lloyd/Flanders
Loloi Rugs
Maitland-Smith
Majestic Mirror
Mark Roberts
Marshall James
Meadowcraft
Michael Thomas
Miles Talbott
Mobel
Mohawk
Motioncraft
Murray Feiss Lighting
Mystic Valley Traders
NDI
Olympia
Palatial Leather
Paragon Picture
Paul Robert
Pawley's Island
Pergo
Possible Dreams

Precedent
Quoizel
Ragno Porcelain
Ralph Lauren
Randall-Allan
Regency Leather
Saloom
Sedgefield By Adams
Serta
Seven Seas Seating
Shadow Catchers
Shaw Flooring
Sherrill
Sligh
Southhampton
Southwood
Spanish Imports
Stanford
Sweet Dreams Linens
Taracea
Taylor King
Theodore Alexander
Timeworks
Toepperwein's
Tommy Bahama
Tradewinds
Treasure Garden
Tropitone
Tyndale
Uttermost
Uwharrie Chair
Venture By Lane
Wesley Allen
West Brothers
Whittemore-Sherrill
Wildwood Lamps
Winners Only
Woodard Furniture

Green Front Furniture (Raleigh) ★★★

2004 Yonkers Road, Raleigh, NC, 20166

Hours: Monday-Saturday 10:00-6:00, Sunday1:00-5:00
Phone: 919-754-9754
Email: greenfrontnc@greenfront.com
Website: greenfront.com
Discount: 40%-50% off mfr retail
Payment: VISA, MasterCard, Discover, Personal Check
Delivery: White glove delivery

This is Green Front Furniture's newest store. They have a very nice selection of medium to high-end lines, including Lexington, Hooker, Sherrill, and Maitland-Smith.

All of Green Front's floor samples and discontinued styles from their three stores and their phone sales service are all sent to their clearance center at their other location in Farmville, VA. For this reason, there is no monetary advantage to shopping at this location in person.

Green Front has a spotless record with the BBB for their Raleigh store, with zero complaints recorded as of this writing in February 2016. I confidently recommend them as a reliable source.

Vendor carries 135 manufacturer's lines

A & B	Bayne	CTH Sherrill Occasional
A.P. Industries	Big Fish Art	Currey & Co.
Allstate	Bradington Young	Custom Shoppe
Althorp Living History	Carver's Guild	David Michael
Art Gallery	Century Furniture	Denny Lamps
Art In Motion	Chinese Imports	Down Right
Arthur Court	Colonial Furniture	Duckworth Fine Arts
Artistica Metal Designs	Columbia	Durham Furniture
Asian Imports	Congoleum	E.J.Victor
Austin Productions	Cooper Classics	Eastern Accents
Barcalounger	Craftmaster Furniture	Elite Manufacturing

Epic Leather
Fanimation
Ferguson Copeland
FFDM
Formica
Four Seasons
Frederick Cooper
Friedman Brothers
GKI
Global Views, Inc.
Habersham
Hanamint
Hancock & Moore
Harden
Hekman
Henkel Harris
Henredon
Henry Link
Hickory Chair
Highland House
Home Source
Hooker
Howard Miller
Huntington House
Interlude
Jason Scott Collection
Jessica Charles
John-Richard
Jonathan Charles
K & K Interiors
Karndean Tile
KAS
King Hickory
Kingsley-Bate

Lane
Laneventure
Leathercraft
Legacy Leather
Leisters Furniture
Lexington
Lloyd/Flanders
Loloi Rugs
Maitland-Smith
Majestic Mirror
Mark Roberts
Marshall James
Meadowcraft
Michael Thomas
Miles Talbott
Mobel
Mohawk
Motioncraft
Murray Feiss Lighting
Mystic Valley Traders
NDI
Olympia
Palatial Leather
Paragon Picture
Paul Robert
Pawley's Island
Pergo
Pinehurst Umbrellas
Possible Dreams
Precedent
Quoizel
Ragno Porcelain
Ralph Lauren
Randall-Allan

Regency Leather
Saloom
Sedgefield By Adams
Serta
Seven Seas Seating
Shadow Catchers
Shaw Flooring
Sherrill
Sligh
Southhampton
Southwood
Spanish Imports
Stanford
Sweet Dreams Linens
Taracea
Taylor King
Theodore Alexander
Timeworks
Toepperwein's
Tommy Bahama
Tradewinds
Treasure Garden
Tropitone
Tyndale
Uttermost
Uwharrie Chair
Venture By Lane
Wesley Allen
West Brothers
Whittemore-Sherrill
Wildwood Lamps
Winners Only
Woodard Furniture
Zimmerman

Grindstaff's Interiors ★★★★

1007 W. Main St., Forest City, NC, 28043

Hours: Monday-Saturday 9:00-6:00
Phone: 828-245-4263
Email: sales@grindstaffs.com
Website: grindstaffs.com
Discount: 35%-50% off mfr retail
Payment: Personal Check
Delivery: White glove delivery

Grindstaff's Interiors is located in Forest City, NC, about an hour southwest of Hickory, NC. They have a beautiful 80,000 square foot store with a good selection of high-end lines, including Baker, Century, and Maitland Smith.

On a recent visit, I found a great bargain on a sofa floor sample from Henredon in new, first-quality condition (pictured on the next page). The retail on this sofa is $7,005.00, but you could purchase this sofa from Grindstaff's for $3,305.00. That's a savings of $3,700.00, or 53% off retail!

Grindstaff's also has a good reputation for service. I've never heard a single complaint about them, and their record with the BBB is very good. As of this writing in February 2016, the BBB gives them an A+ rating with only one resolved complaint in the last three years. They've been family owned since 1956. The current owner is Boyce Grindstaff.

If you are traveling here in person, please be aware that the store is in a small town about 1 hour and 15 minutes away from either Hickory or Asheville. Unless you are staying overnight in town, please consider leaving Forest City at least a couple of hours before sundown. The roads back to the more populated areas where most travelers would stay are very dark at night and can be confusing for out of town shoppers.

While the showroom here is beautiful and the staff is very helpful, Grindstaff's is way off the beaten path for most travelers. I don't find that the extra discounts available in person justify the additional driving time to go to Grindstaff's in person. Most shoppers would be better off just to call them for a comparison quote.

Henredon sofa at Grindstaff's Interiors

Retail: $7,005.00 Discounted price: $3,305.00
Savings at Grindstaff's Interiors: $3,700.00 = 53% off retail

Vendor carries 54 manufacturer's lines

Ambella Home	Frederick Cooper	Magnussen Home
American Drew	Hammary	Maitland-Smith
Baker Furniture	Hanamint	Martha Stewart
Bassett	Hancock & Moore	Meadowcraft
Bassett Baby/Juvenile	Hekman	Milling Road
Bassett Mirror	Henredon	Motioncraft
Bernhardt	Hickory Chair	Palliser
Bradington Young	Hickory White	Pulaski
Century Furniture	Hooker	Randall-Allan
Charleston Forge	Howard Miller	Sherrill
Cox Manufacturing Co	Jessica Charles	Southwood
Craftique	John-Richard	Stein World
CTH Sherrill Occasional	Karastan	Temple
Distinctive Designs	Kincaid	Theodore Alexander
Drexel Heritage	King Hickory	Thomasville
Fairfield Chair	La Barge	Wesley Allen
Fashion Bed Group	Lexington	Woodard Furniture
FFDM	Lloyd/Flanders	Woodmark Furniture

Harden Factory Outlet ★★★★★

Mill Pond Way, McConnellsville, NY, 13401

Hours: Monday-Saturday 10:00-5:00
Phone: 315-245-1000
Email: None
Website: harden.com
Discount: 50%-75% off mfr retail
Payment: VISA, MasterCard, American Express, Personal Check
Delivery: Free delivery to the Harden dealer closest to buyer's home

This is Harden Furniture's only factory outlet, located in the Harden factory itself in McConnellsville, NY, near Oneida Lake just east of Syracuse, NY. Actually, the outlet is what they call an "overpile" room, where they store photography samples, seconds, floor samples, discontinued styles, and overruns.

Most of the stock here is solid cherry case goods. This is a very high-quality traditional furniture line. The discounts here run from 50%-75% off retail.

Harden conducts business a bit differently from most outlets. If you come by to look through their overpile room, and you find something you like, they won't allow you to buy it on the spot. They tag it and ship it free of charge to the Harden dealer nearest you on the next Harden truck delivering furniture to that particular store. This can take up to a month. Then, when it arrives at your local Harden dealer, you'll be notified to come pick it up and pay the dealer for it directly. You do still pay the outlet price however.

If you plan to stop by this outlet, you may wish to plan your visit on a Wednesday morning. The Harden factory gives one-hour factory tours every Wednesday at 10:00. It's quite interesting, and it's free.

This is a good source. Harden has very high-quality gorgeous furniture, and the prices are quite good.

...on Factory Outlet ★★★★★

Furniture Mart - U. S. Hwy 70 SE, Level 1, Hickory, NC, 28602

Hours: Monday-Saturday 9:00-6:00
Phone: 828-322-7111
Email: info@hickoryfurniture.com
Website: henredon.com
Discount: 60%-70% off mfr retail
Payment: VISA, MasterCard, Personal Check
Delivery: White glove delivery

The Henredon Factory Outlet at the Hickory Furniture Mart has a huge selection of Henredon case goods and upholstery. This is the only factory outlet left for Henredon now that their other outlet in High Point has closed.

Most of the pieces here are floor samples and discontinued items, although there are some seconds. Even the seconds have extremely small flaws, however. The discounts are very good: 60%-70% off retail.

On a recent visit, I found a wonderful deal on a Henredon "Lenora" sofa (left) in new first-quality condition. This sofa retails for $12,537.00, but you could buy this sofa from the outlet for only $5,649.00. That's a savings of $6,888.00, or 55% off retail.

This outlet normally has sales in February, May, and November, when all items are marked down an extra 10%-20%, so you may wish to consider this in making your travel plans to North Carolina. Many other outlets and showrooms have special sales in February, May, and November as well.

The outlet will not special order new Henredon furniture, but if you see a Henredon piece you like at a local furniture store, you can call the outlet to see if they might have a floor sample or a similar discontinued style. The outlet will take these types of orders by phone and have your furniture shipped to you.

Anyone considering purchasing Henredon furniture should definitely check this outlet out before they buy, preferably in person. This outlet is a "must-visit".

"Lenora" sofa at the Henredon Factory Outlet

Retail: $12,537.00 Discounted price: $5,649.00
Savings at the Henredon Factory Outlet: $6,888.00 = 55% off retail

Vendor carries 1 manufacturer's lines

Henredon

Heritage Furniture Outlet ★★★★★

Hickory Furniture Mart - U. S. Hwy 70 SE, Level 3 & 4, Hickory, NC, 28602

Hours: Monday-Saturday 9:00-6:00
Phone: 828-855-2950
Email: regina@heritagefurnitureoutlet.com
Website: heritagefurnitureoutlet.com
Discount: 40%-60% off mfr retail
Payment: VISA, MasterCard, American Express, Discover, Personal Check
Delivery: White glove delivery

Heritage Furniture Outlet at the Hickory Furniture Mart sells market samples, closeouts, and discontinued furniture from many high-end brands: Schnadig, Charleston Forge, Council Craftsmen, Burton James, Fine Furniture Designs (FFDM), HFI, Hickory Heritage, Panama Jack, Palmetto Home, King Koil Bedding, Legacy Outdoor, Miles Talbot, and Overnight Mattresses.

On a recent visit, I found a great deal on a Panama Jack king bedroom set from Palmetto Home (pictured on the next page). The bed shown retails for $1,400.00, but you could buy this one at the Heritage Furniture Outlet for only $699.00. That's a savings of $701.00, or 50% off retail. It was in new first-quality condition.

The Heritage Furniture Outlet is owned by the same company that owns the Hooker Furniture Outlet next door at the Mart. Both showrooms are very reputable and have excellent service.

This is a great source! A must visit!

Vendor carries 10 manufacturer's lines

Burton James	FFDM	Miles Talbot
Charleston Forge	Hickory Heritage	Overnight Mattresses
Clayton Marcus	King Koil	
Council Craftsmen	Legacy Outdoor	

Panama Jack bed at Heritage Furniture Outlet

Retail: $1,400.00 Discounted price: $699.00
Savings at Heritage Furniture Outlet: $701.00 = 50% off retail

Hickory Furniture Mart

★★★★★

U. S. Hwy 70 SE, Hickory, NC, 28602

Hours: Monday-Saturday 9:00-6:00
Phone: 828-322-3510 / 800-462-MART
Email: info@hickoryfurniture.com
Website: hickoryfurniture.com

The Hickory Furniture Mart has some excellent deals from legitimate discounters and true factory outlets, including factory authorized factory outlets for Hooker, Maitland-Smith, Henredon, Mitchell Gold (Pottery Barn), Designmaster, Distinction Leather, Drexel Heritage, Hickory White, Highland House, Century, La Barge, Hollin Gate, Southern Style, Vanguard, and Wesley Hall. Over half a million visitors come here to shop every year.

All of the tenants currently occupying the Mart have good reputations for service. Prices may vary among the various showrooms and outlets, even on identical items, so do shop around carefully during your visit.

Many discounters and outlets at the Mart have special sales in May and November, right after the semi-annual High Point International Home Furnishings Market, as well as in February and July when business is traditionally slow. Many other factory outlets and showrooms all over North Carolina have special sales during these months, too, so you may wish to plan any trips to take advantage of these extra discounts.

The Mart has two small restaurants: Taste Full Beans (828-328-6099) and Grapevines (828-324-7204). Each offers sandwiches, coffee, etc. Taste Full Beans on Level 1 also has free wireless internet service.

Designing Women at the Mart (828-328-5200) offers guided tours of the Mart and detailed design assistance from licensed interior designers by appointment. The Mart itself also offers a complimentary decorating service to clients who are furnishing two or more rooms.

Please see the individual listings in this book for each discounter or outlet for details on payment, shipping, lines carried, etc. If you plan to visit Hickory, you may wish to plan your trip around the Mart sale weekends so that you can shop on Sunday if you wish. Most stores in this area are closed on Sunday during the rest of the year.

Amish Oak & Cherry	828-261-4776
Comfort Zone by Hickory Park	828-326-9224
Distinctive Furnishings of Hickory	828-455-6062
Flexsteel Signature Gallery	828-322-3532
Good's Home Furnishings	828-322-3471
Henredon Factory Outlet	828-322-7111
Heritage Furniture Outlet	828-855-2950
Hickory Outlet Center	828-256-0003
Hickory Park Furniture Galleries	828-322-4440
Hickory White Factory Outlet	828-327-3766
Hooker Factory Outlet	828-855-2950
Leather & More	828-324-0668
Maitland-Smith Factory Outlet	828-322-7111
Mitchell Gold + Bob Williams Outlet	828-261-0051
Reflections	828-327-8485
Southern Style Furniture	828-322-7000
Southern Style Fine Furniture Outlet	828-855-2252
Vanguard Factory Outlet	828-322-3471

Hickory Outlet Center ★★★★★

Hickory Furniture Mart - U. S. Hwy 70 SE, Level 2, Hickory, NC, 28602

Hours: Monday-Saturday 9:00-6:00
Phone: 828-256-0003
Email: info@hickoryoutletcenter.com
Website: hickoryoutletcenter.com
Discount: 50%-60% off mfr retail
Payment: VISA, MasterCard, American Express, Discover, Personal Check
Delivery: White glove delivery

Hickory Outlet Center is one of the newest factory outlets in the Hickory area. They are the authorized factory outlet for many high-end brands: Maitland-Smith, Drexel Heritage, Designmaster Furniture, Distinction Leather, Sarreid, Ltd., Wesley Hall, Lane Venture, Stanford Furniture, and Hollin Gate.

They stock market samples, showroom samples, and discontinued styles at "factory direct prices to the public". Usually, that means at least 50%-60% off retail. Most of the furniture here is in excellent condition, having only been shown at private trade showrooms.

On a recent visit, I found a great deal here on a hand-painted Chinoiserie table from Maitland-Smith in new, first-quality condition (pictured on the next page). The table retailed for $2,798.00, but you could buy this one at the outlet for only $1,119.00! That's a savings of $1,679.00, or 60% off retail!

The Hickory Outlet Center has excellent service. They have no complaints whatsoever recorded with the BBB, and I've never heard a single complaint about them from my readers.

They have some incredible deals here. I highly recommend this source!

Vendor carries 9 manufacturer's lines

Designmaster	Hollin Gate	Stanford
Distinction Leather	Maitland-Smith	Venture By Lane
Drexel Heritage	Sarreid	Wesley Hall

102

Maitland-Smith table at Hickory Outlet Center

Retail: $2,798.00 Discounted price: $1,119.00
Savings at Hickory Outlet Center: $1,679.00 = 60% off retail

Hickory Park Furniture Galleries ★★★★

Hickory Furniture Mart - U. S. Hwy 70 SE, Levels 2, 3, & 4, Hickory, NC, 28602

Hours: Monday-Saturday 9:00-6:00
Phone: 828-322-4440
Email: hparksales@hickorypark.com
Website: hickorypark.com
Discount: 40%-50% off mfr retail
Payment: VISA, MasterCard, American Express, Personal Check
Delivery: White glove delivery

Hickory Park has dedicated showrooms at the Hickory Furniture Mart for Bassett, La-Z-Boy, Kincaid, Hickory Chair, Hancock & Moore, Broyhill, Rowe and Lane. They also have showrooms dedicated to home office furniture, outdoor furniture, leather furniture and reclining furniture. Their prices tend to run 40%-50% off retail.

For example, on a recent visit I found a beautiful cherry queen bed from Cresent (pictured on the next page) for only $799.00 during their after market sale! This bed retails for $1,499.00. That's a 47% savings on a new bed in flawless condition!

Their "Comfort Zone" showroom specializes in leather, upholstery, sectionals, and recliners. It also has some unique products, such as zero gravity recliners and massage chairs from Interactive Health.

In March 2013, Hickory Park opened a new Flexsteel gallery at the Hickory Furniture Mart to replace the gallery vacated by Tarheel Home Furnishings. Hickory Park is now the only authorized Flexsteel dealer in the greater Hickory, NC, area.

Hickory Park also has a new clearance center in the Hickory Furniture Mart with even better bargains! Most of the furniture in stock is marked about 60% off retail.

Hickory Park has an A+ with the BBB, and I have no complaints on file about them from any of my readers. If you plan to special order any of the lines below by phone, you should definitely call them for a price quote. I have always found Hickory Park to be a reputable source with excellent customer service during the thirty years they've been in business. I highly recommend them as a source!

Cherry queen bed by Cresent at Hickory Park Furniture Galleries
Retail: $1,499.00 Discounted price: $799.00
Savings at Hickory Park Furniture Galleries: $700.00 = 47% off retail

Vendor carries 76 manufacturer's lines

Action by Lane
American Drew
Artitalia Group
Bassett
Bob Timberlake
Broyhill
C. R. Laine Upholstery
Cambridge Mills
Canadel
Caracole
Century Furniture
Charleston Forge
Classic Home
Classic Leather
Comfort Designs
Company C
Compositions By Schnadig
Councill
Cozzia Furniture
Cresent
Curations Limited
Cyan Design
Durham Furniture
Eastern Accents
Eastern Legends
Fairfield Chair

Flat Rock Furniture
Flexsteel
Furniture Classics Ltd.
Gloster
Guildmaster
Hammary
Hancock & Moore
Harden
Hekman
Hickory at Home
Hickory Chair
IMG
Interlude
Jasper Cabinet
Jessica Charles
Kincaid
La-Z-Boy
Lane
Laneventure
Legacy Classic
Legacy Linens
Legends Furniture
Lloyd/Flanders
Mikhail Darafeev
Old Biscayne Designs
Old Hickory Tannery

Orient Express Furniture
Paladin
Parker Southern
Port Eliot
Randall-Allan
Riverside Furniture
Riverwood
Rizzy Home
Robin Bruce
Rowe Furniture
Schnadig
Shadow Mountain
Sit Strong Systems
Spring Air
Style Upholstery
Swaim
Tempur-pedic
Timmerman
Tropitone
Uttermost
Wesley Allen
Whitecraft Rattan
Winners Only
Woodard Furniture

Hickory White Factory Outlet ★★★★★

Hickory Furniture Mart - U. S. Hwy 70 SE, Level 4, Hickory, NC, 28602

Hours: Monday-Saturday 9:00-6:00
Phone: 828-327-3766
Email: info@hickoryfurniture.com
Website: hickorywhite.com
Discount: 50%-75% off mfr retail
Payment: VISA, MasterCard, Personal Check
Delivery: White glove delivery

The Hickory White Factory Outlet at the Hickory Furniture Mart has a fair selection of upholstery and case goods. It's the only factory outlet left for this brand. The Hickory White factory outlets in Burlington, NC, and Commerce, GA, have both closed.

Most of the pieces here are floor samples and discontinued items. The discounts are very good: 50%-75% off retail, with most first quality pieces running about 55%-60% off retail. They also have a very nice selection of furniture and accessories from sister brand Theodore Alexander displayed at the same location.

For example, I found a beautiful trompe l'oeil bookcase at this outlet on a recent visit (pictured on the following page). The retail on this bookcase is $2,055.00, but you can buy this one at the outlet for only $899.00, a savings of 56% off retail! It had no flaws I could find.

This outlet normally has sales in February, May, July, and November, when all items are marked down an extra 10%-20%, so you may wish to consider this in making your travel plans to North Carolina. Many other outlets and showrooms have special sales in February, May, and November as well.

Anyone considering purchasing Hickory White furniture should definitely check this outlet out before they buy. This outlet is a "must-visit".

Trompe l'oeil bookcase at the Hickory White Factory Outlet

Retail: $2,055.00 Discounted price: $899.00
Savings at the Hickory White Factory Outlet: $1,156.00 = 56% off retail

High Point Furniture Sales

★★★★

2000 Baker Rd., High Point, NC, 27260

Hours: Monday-Friday 9:00-5:30,
Saturday 9:00-4:30
Phone: 336-841-5664 / 800-334-1875
Email: Kent@HighPointFurnitureSales.com
Website: highpointfurnituresales.com
Discount: 40%-50% off mfr retail
Payment: Personal Check
Delivery: White glove delivery

High Point Furniture Sales offers over 100 lines at 40%-50% off retail. They have a beautiful showroom right off the Baker Rd. exit on Business I-85.

On a recent visit, I found a good deal on a sofa and chairs by C. R. Laine (pictured on the following page). Retail on this group is $4,693.00, but you could special order the same set in a variety of colors for only $2,856.00, a savings of 40% off retail.

This store usually gives an extra 5% off furniture purchased off the floor if you know to ask. The staff here is very helpful, and the store has a long reputation for excellent service.

As of this writing in February 2016, they have an A+ rating with the BBB, with only one complaint in the last three years. I highly recommend them as a source.

C. R. Laine living room set at High Point Furniture Sales

Retail: $4,693.00 Discounted price: $2,856.00
Savings at High Point Furniture Sales: $1,837.00 = 40% off retail

Vendor carries 116 manufacturer's lines

A-America	Bradington Young	Cochrane Furniture
Action by Lane	Brass Craft	Cox Manufacturing Co
Aico (Michael Amini)	Braxton Culler	Crawford of Jamestown
American Drew	Broyhill	Crystal Clear Industries
American Mirror	C. R. Laine Upholstery	Decorative Crafts
Ashley Furniture	Cambridge Lamps	Designmaster
Austin Sculpture	Cape Craftsmen	Dillon
Baldwin Clocks	Capris Furniture	Distinctive Designs
Barcalounger	Carolina Mirror	Douglas
Bassett	Casual Lamps	Dutailier
Beachcraft Mfg.	Cebu Furniture	Fabricoate
Benicia Foundry	Chromcraft	Fashion Bed Group
Berkline	Classic Rattan	Ficks Reed

Fine Art Lamps
Floral Art
Frederick Cooper
Friedman Brothers
Friendship Upholstery
Great American
Great City Traders
Greene Brothers
Guildmaster
Hammary
Hekman
Henry Link
High Point Furniture
Hollywoods
Homelegance
Howard Miller
Jeffco
Johnston Casuals
Kathy Ireland
Kincaid
Lane
Laneventure
Lea Industries
Leisters Furniture
Lexington
Lloyd/Flanders

Lyon Shaw
Magnussen Home
Master Design
Mikhail Darafeev
Mobel
Nichols & Stone
Null Furniture
Ohio Table Pad
Oriental Lacquer
Palecek
Paragon Picture
Park Place
Parker House
Peters-Revington
Phillips Furniture
Pieri Creations
Plant Plant
Pulaski
Regency House
Remington Lamp
Ridgeway Clocks
Riverside Furniture
Rowe Furniture
Rug Barn
Sam Moore
San Diego Design

Schnadig
Sealy
Serta
Signature Rugs
Standard
Stein World
Stiffel Lamps
Taylorsville
Telescope
Therapedic Bedding
Timeless Bedding
Tropitone
Universal Furniture
Uttermost
Uwharrie Chair
Van Teal
Vaughan Bassett
Vaughan Furniture
Venture By Lane
Victorian Classics
Wesley Allen
Wesley Hall
Wildwood Lamps
Winston
Woodard Furniture

High Point Furniture Sales Clearance ★★★★

2035 Brentwood Street, High Point, NC, 27260

Hours: Monday-Friday 9:00-5:30,
Saturday 9:00-4:30
Phone: 336-841-5664 / 800-334-1875
Email: Contact@HighPointFurnitureSales.com
Website: highpointfurnituresales.com
Discount: 60%-70% off mfr retail
Payment: Personal Check
Delivery: White glove delivery

High Point Furniture Sales Clearance is right up Business I-85 from their main showroom on Baker Rd. The clearance center has some quite good deals on a wide variety of the lines carried by the main showroom.

Please see the listing in this book for High Point Furniture Sales for a full listing of the lines they carry. Most of the items at the clearance center are floor samples, discontinued styles, and customer returns. The majority are in new first-quality condition.

For example, on a recent visit, I found a great deal on an armoire by Hooker Furniture, pictured on the following page. The retail on this piece is $1,838.00, but you could buy this one for only $699.00, a savings of 62% of retail. It was in very good condition.

High Point Furniture Sales has an excellent reputation for customer service, and some very good bargains. If you are traveling to High Point in person to shop, this clearance center is well worth a visit.

Armoire from Hooker Furniture

Retail: $1,838.00 Discounted price: $699.00
Savings at High Point Furniture Sales Clearance: $1,139.00 = 62% off retail

High Point Home Furnishings Center ★★★

1100 Trinity Ave., High Point, NC, 27260

Hours: Monday-Saturday 10:00-5:00, Sunday 12:00-4:00
Phone: 336-887-7477
Email: showrooms@highpointcenter.com
Website: highpointcenter.com
Discount: 40%-50% off mfr retail
Payment: VISA, MasterCard, Discover, Personal Check
Delivery: White glove delivery

The High Point Home Furnishings Center is owned by Gonzalez & Associates, a Mexican manufacturer of rustic pine furniture and leather upholstery. If you're decorating a cabin or a Southwestern style home, this is a great place to shop. Please note that this showroom is closed to the public during all of April and October due to the wholesale home furnishings market in High Point.

You can also find galleries for three other lines here: Furniture Traditions manufactures very good quality solid oak traditional furniture in simple American styles. Southern Dreams manufactures medium quality upholstery. Therapedic Bedding manufactures high end mattresses.

The High Point Home Furnishings Center is a major provider of warehousing, shipping, and container packing services for manufacturers and furniture discounters. I've hired them myself to pack containers for overseas clients. I've always been very happy with their services.

The owner, Eric Gonzalez, is honest and reputable. I've never heard a single complaint about any of his companies. If you're in the area, I certainly recommend that you stop in, especially if you're looking for rustic furniture.

Vendor carries 4 manufacturer's lines

Furniture Traditions	Southern Dreams
Gonzalez & Associates	Therapedic Bedding

Hollin Gate

★★★★★

4141 York View Ct., Granite Falls, NC, 28630

Hours: Friday-Saturday 10:00-5:00, Sunday1:00-5:00
Phone: 828-324-9400
Email: info@hollingate.com
Website: hollingate.com
Discount: 50%-70% off mfr retail
Payment: VISA, MasterCard, American Express, Discover, Personal Check
Delivery: Full service in-home delivery and set-up. Customer pays freight directly.

In 2013, Hollin Gate bought Boulevard Bazaar, the Century Furniture Factory Outlet in Charlotte, NC. Now, the only two factory outlets for Century and their affiliated brands are Hollin Gate in Granite Falls, NC, and the Century Factory Outlet at the Hickory Furniture Mart in Hickory, NC.

On a recent visit I found an excellent deal on a Century leather chair (pictured on the following page). It retails for $3,348.00, but you could buy this floor sample for only $1,339.00, a savings of 60% off retail. It had no flaws I could find.

Most of the furniture in stock is from Century Furniture and their sister brand, Heritage House. Both lines are still manufactured entirely in the U. S., a few miles down the road in Hickory, NC. You'll also find discontinued items and overstocks from Drexel Heritage, Maitland-Smith, Woodbridge, and Hollin Gate. Virtually all of the furniture here is in new first-quality condition.

Hollin Gate has a terrific selection of overstock and remnant fabric from Century at about 60% off retail across the board. Most fabrics are $8/yard if you purchase custom cut yardage. Small remnants (1-2 yards typically) run $4/yard.

Hollin Gate also has some very nice deals on grandfather clocks, statuary, marble fountains, and other decorative accessories. If you plan to pick up a grandfather clock while shopping for furniture in North Carolina, this is one of the very best sources you will find.

This is a very reputable store, and the outlet pieces from Century are well-priced. I've known owner Kelly McGrath for many years, and he runs an honest company with knowledgable staff. The customer service here is excellent. If

115

you're in the Hickory area shopping for grandfather clocks or traditional furniture, I highly recommend you stop in.

Century leather chair at Hollin Gate

Retail: $3,348.00 Discounted price: $1,339.00
Savings at Hollin Gate: $2,009.00 = 60% off retail

Vendor carries 6 manufacturer's lines

Century Furniture	Highland House	Maitland-Smith
Drexel Heritage	Hollin Gate	Woodbridge

Homeway Furniture

121 W. Lebanon St., Mount Airy, NC, 27030

Hours: Monday-Friday 9:00-5:30, Saturday 9:00-5:00
Phone: 336-786-6151 / 800-334-9094
Email: homeway@homewayfurniture.com
Website: homewayfurniture.com
Discount: 40%-50% off mfr retail
Payment: VISA, MasterCard, American Express, Discover, Personal Check
Delivery: White glove delivery

Homeway Furniture is located in Mt. Airy, NC, about an hour's drive north of High Point, NC. They have a very nice selection of high end lines, including Bradington Young, Hooker, and Maitland-Smith.

Prices here typically run 40%-50% off retail. They have a spotless record of customer service. As of this writing in February 2016, they have an A+ rating with the BBB. I've never heard a single reader complaint about them.

I highly recommend this source!

Vendor carries 103 manufacturer's lines

A.P. Industries	Classic Leather	Flexsteel
Acacia Furniture	Classic Rattan	Furniture Classics Ltd.
American Drew	Clayton Marcus	Gat Creek
Aspen Furniture	Clearwater American	Hammary
Bassett	Cox Manufacturing Co	Hekman
Bassett Mirror	Craftmaster Furniture	Hillsdale Barstools
Bemco	CTH Sherrill Occasional	Holland House
Better Homes	Denny Lamps	Homelegance
Bradington Young	Dutailier	Hooker
Braxton Culler	East End Imports	Howard Miller
Broyhill	Fairfield Chair	Joffran
Butler Specialty	Fairmont Designs	John Thomas Furniture
Canadel	Fashion Bed Group	Johnston Casuals
Capel Rugs	FFDM	Key City Furniture

Kincaid	Palliser	Stein World
King Hickory	Paula Deen Home	Summer Classics
Kingsdown	Pembrook	Temple
Klaussner	Penns Creek	Tennessee Enterprises
Lane	Pennsylvania House	Tom Seely Furniture
Largo	Peters-Revington	Troutman Chair
Lea Industries	Powell	Ultimate Accents
Legacy Classic	Primo	Universal Furniture
Legends Furniture	Progressive Furniture	USA Premium Leather
Leisters Furniture	Pulaski	Uttermost
Liberty	Restonic	Uwharrie Chair
Lloyd/Flanders	Ridgeway Clocks	Vaughan Bassett
MacKenzie Dow	Riverside Furniture	Vaughan Furniture
Magnussen Home	Rowe Furniture	Vineyard Furniture
Maitland-Smith	Saloom	Wesley Allen
Mobel	Sam Moore	Wesley Hall
New River Artisans	Samuel Lawrence	Whitewood Interiors
Oriental Weavers	Schnadig	Winners Only
Overnight Sofas	Seven Seas Seating	Wynwood
Paladin	Shadow Mountain	
Palecek	Signature Designs	

Hooker Factory Outlet   ★★★★★

Hickory Furniture Mart - U. S. Hwy 70 SE, Level 4, Hickory, NC, 28602

Hours: Monday-Saturday 9:00-6:00
Phone: 828-855-2950
Email: hookerfurnitureoutlet@gmail.com
Website: hookerfurnitureoutlet.com
Discount: 40%-60% off mfr retail
Payment: VISA, MasterCard, American Express, Discover, Personal Check
Delivery: White glove delivery

Hooker Factory Outlet at the Hickory Furniture Mart sells market samples, closeouts, and discontinued furniture from Hooker Furniture and Seven Seas Seating, both very high end lines.

Here's a great example of what they offer. This beautiful executive desk from Hooker (pictured on the following page) retails for $2,802.00, but you can buy the same desk in first quality condition at the factory outlet for only $1,096.00! That's a savings of 61% off retail!

The Hooker Furniture Outlet is owned by the same company that owns the Heritage Furniture Outlet next door at the Mart. Both showrooms are very reputable and have excellent service.

This is a great source! A must visit!

Vendor carries 2 manufacturer's lines

Hooker   Seven Seas Seating

Executive desk with hutch from Hooker Furniture

Retail: $2,966.00 Discounted price: $1,199.00
Savings at Hooker Factory Outlet: $1,767.00 = 60% off retail

Hooker Furniture Factory Outlet   ★★★★★

115 East Church Street, Martinsville, VA, 24112

Hours: Monday-Saturday 10:00-6:00
Phone: 276-638-2040
Email: hookeroutlet@hotmail.com
Website: hookerfurniture.com
Discount: 60%-70% off mfr retail
Payment: VISA, MasterCard, American Express, Discover, Personal Check
Delivery: White glove delivery

The Hooker Furniture Outlet in Martinsville, VA is about an hour's drive north of High Point, and worth every minute of the drive. The majority of the stock at this outlet is new and in first-quality condition. Most pieces are 65% off retail.

The Hooker Furniture Outlet has moved two doors down from its former location. It is now located inside Martin Plaza, making room for a new Darlee Outdoor Furniture Outlet in its former location. Other than that, nothing has changed.

This outlet is now the only U. S. factory outlet for Bassett Furniture, which is also discounted about 65% off retail.

The staff is great to work with. Unlike most factory outlets, this one will take phone orders. If there is a certain item you want from Hooker or Bassett, just check the manufacturer's online catalog and call the outlet to see if they have one in stock. If they do, they'll be happy to take your order over the phone.

Hooker is best known for their entertainment centers and armoires, which make up the majority of the stock here. You will also find some nice marble-topped bathroom vanities, dining room sets, home office furniture, and even pieces from Hookers brand new line of childrens furniture.

On a recent visit, I found a great deal on a beautiful hand painted armoire (pictured on the following page). It retails for $3,147.00, but you could buy this one for only $999.00. That's a 68% discount! It was in new first quality condition with no flaws. That's a steal for such a beautiful piece!

The Hooker Furniture Outlet is owned by Fred Martin Associates, which also owns the Lane Factory Outlet, Martin Plaza, and The Showroom in Martinsville. They have a great reputation for service. All of the furniture discounters and factory outlets owned by the Martin family have had spotless records with the BBB for many years with no complaints whatsoever. I've always been very pleased with how they've worked with my private clients and shopping tours.

This is a great source. If you plan to visit High Point, you may wish to take a day to drive to the Martinsville, VA area, which also has outlets for Pulaski, Stanley, and Lane, as well as a great clearance center (Martin Plaza). The bargains here are well worth the extra travel time.

Painted armoire from Hooker

Retail: $3,147.00 Discounted price: $999.00
Savings at the Hooker Factory Outlet: $2,148.00 = 68% off retail

In Your Home Furnishings   ★

210 13th St. SW, Hickory, NC, 28602

Hours: Monday-Saturday 10:00-6:00
Phone: 828-304-0741
Email: aharris@shopashley.com
Website: None
Discount: 20% off mfr retail
Payment: VISA, MasterCard, Discover, Personal Check
Delivery: White glove delivery

In Your Home Furnishings has moved to a new location due to the closure of the Catawba Furniture Mall. Their new location is in the former Bonita Home Furnishings building in Hickory, NC. Management has not changed. William and Crystal Hutson are still the owners.

As of this writing in February 2016, this store has 25 complaints on record with the BBB, which is worrisome for a store of this size. The prices here are nothing special, and the salespeople I've met are very pushy and annoying.

I can't recommend that anyone shop here. There are so many other sources nearby in Hickory, NC, with better reputations and better prices.

Vendor carries 16 manufacturer's lines

Ashley Furniture	Kathy Ireland	Serta
Broughton Hall	Luke Leather	Simmons
Broyhill	McNeilly Champion	Stein World
Fairmont Designs	Paula Deen Home	T. S. Berry
Fireside Lodge Furniture	Pelican Reef	
Guildcraft of California	Powell	

Kagans (High Point) ★★

1628 S. Main St., High Point, NC, 27261

Hours: Monday-Saturday 9:30-6:00
Phone: 336-883-7113
Email: See web site
Website: kagansfurnitureonline.com
Discount: 30%-50% off mfr retail
Payment: Personal Check
Delivery: White glove delivery

Kagan's Furniture has an A+ rating with the Better Business Bureau as of this writing in March 2016.

Vendor carries 48 manufacturer's lines

A.A. Importing Company	H Studio	Primo
Aico (Michael Amini)	Highland House	Pulaski
American Drew	Howard Miller	Riverside Furniture
Artmax	Huntington Furniture	Robin Bruce
Ashley Furniture	Johnston Casuals	Rossetto
Bassett Mirror	King Koil	Rowe Furniture
BDI/Becker Designed	Lane	Samuel Lawrence
Broughton Hall	Lazar Industries	Schnadig
Butler Specialty	Leda	Sealy
Clayton Marcus	Lexington	Signature Designs
Cochrane Furniture	Magnussen Home	Sunrise Furniture
Dall Agnese	Master Design	Ultimate Accents
Doimo	Millennium	Universal Furniture
Ello	Palliser	Vaughan Furniture
Excelsior	Peopleloungers	Vineyard Furniture
Fairmont Designs	Philip Reinisch	Winners Only

Kagans (Jamestown) ★★

Furniture Avenue Galleries - 4350 Furniture Ave., Jamestown, NC, 27282

Hours: Tuesday-Saturday 9:30-5:30
Phone: 336-885-8300
Email: See web site
Website: kagansfurnitureonline.com
Discount: 30%-50% off mfr retail
Payment: Personal Check
Delivery: White glove delivery

Kagan's Furniture Galleries has a nice selection of furniture, most of which is priced at 30%-60% off retail. For example, on a recent visit I found this "Palais Royale" bedroom set from AICO. Kagan's Furniture offered this set for $6,288.00, including the king bed, dresser, mirror, and two nightstands.

No retail price was quoted at Kagan's for comparison, so let's compare Kagan's price to one of their national competitors: Wayfair.com.

As of this writing in March 2016, the identical set can be purchased at Wayfair.com for $9,783.00, so the price at Kagan's represents a 36% discount off of Wayfair.com's price.

Kagan's offered the matching armoire shown for $3,258.00. Wayfair.com's price on the identical armoire is $2,728.00, so Kagan's price represents a 16% discount off of Wayfair.com's price.

It's worth noting that Wayfair offers free in-home delivery nationwide on this set, where Kagan's charges extra for delivery. The exact delivery charges will vary depending on where the furniture is being delivered, but it will definitely offset some of the savings.

"Palais Royale" bedroom by AICO at Kagan's Furniture Galleries

Competitor's price (Wayfair.com): $8,222.65 Discounted price: $6,288.00
Savings at Kagan's Furniture Galleries: $1,934.65 = 24% off competitor's price

Vendor carries 48 manufacturer's lines

A.A. Importing Company	H Studio	Primo
Aico (Michael Amini)	Highland House	Pulaski
American Drew	Howard Miller	Riverside Furniture
Artmax	Huntington Furniture	Robin Bruce
Ashley Furniture	Johnston Casuals	Rossetto
Bassett Mirror	King Koil	Rowe Furniture
BDI/Becker Designed	Lane	Samuel Lawrence
Broughton Hall	Lazar Industries	Schnadig
Butler Specialty	Leda	Sealy
Clayton Marcus	Lexington	Signature Designs
Cochrane Furniture	Magnussen Home	Sunrise Furniture
Dall Agnese	Master Design	Ultimate Accents
Doimo	Millennium	Universal Furniture
Ello	Palliser	Vaughan Furniture
Excelsior	Peopleloungers	Vineyard Furniture
Fairmont Designs	Philip Reinisch	Winners Only

Kincaid Factory Outlet ★★★★★

Manufacturer-Owned Factory Outlets, 4916 Hickory Blvd, Hickory, NC, 28601

Hours: Monday-Saturday 9:00-6:00, Sunday1:00-5:00
Phone: 828-496-2262
Email: None
Website: kincaidfurniture.com
Discount: 50%-75% off mfr retail
Payment: VISA, MasterCard, Personal Check
Delivery: White glove delivery

This is Kincaid's only true factory outlet, in the Manufacturer-Owned Factory Outlets just north of Hickory, NC. This outlet is considerably larger than Kincaid's former factory outlet in Lenoir. It has a very nice selection of case goods and upholstery.

This outlet also serves as a factory outlet for La-Z-Boy, which owns Kincaid Furniture, so there an area toward the back with La-Z-Boy chairs and recliners.

There are virtually no seconds here. Most of the items in stock are floor samples from the semi-annual wholesale furniture markets in High Point and discontinued styles.

On a recent visit here, I found a great deal on a Laura Ashley dining room set by Kincaid. The regular retail on the table, four side chairs, two arm chairs, and the china cabinet is $6,552.00, but the regular outlet price on this set was only $2,841.00, a savings of 57% off retail.

Plus, because I visited during their semi-annual after market sale, this set was marked down an additional 10% to $2,098.00, a savings of 67% off retail! It was in first quality condition with no flaws I could see. This outlet also holds an after market sale twice each year in early May and early November. Please check www.smartdecorating.com for current sale dates.

Vendor carries 3 manufacturer's lines

Kincaid   La-Z-Boy   Laura Ashley

Laura Ashley dining room set from Kincaid

Retail: $6,552.00 Discounted price: $2,098.00
Savings at the Kincaid Factory Outlet: $4,454.00 = 67% off retail

King Hickory Furniture Outlet

★★★★★

728 Highland Ave., Hickory, NC, 28601

Hours: Monday-Saturday 10:00-4:00
Phone: 828-324-0472
Email: None
Website: kinghickory.com
Discount: 25% to 35% off wholesale prices
Payment: Personal Check
Delivery: Nationwide via third party carrier

The King Hickory Furniture Outlet Store is an excellent source for American made upholstery. The outlet is connected to King Hickory's #2 upholstery factory in downtown Hickory, NC. Their quality is very good: 8 way hand-tied springs, hardwood frames, etc.

The outlet does a brisk business. During my last visit, the manager told me she'd sold 11 sofas just that morning. This is a popular destination for interior designers in the know all over the Southeast.

On a recent visit, I found a great deal on a red leather "Athens" chair with ottoman (pictured on the next page). The wholesale price to furniture stores is $1,234.90, but you could get this chair at the outlet for $799.00. That's a savings of $435.90, or 35% off wholesale.

All of the furniture at this outlet is marked as a discount off of the wholesale price to furniture stores, not as a discount off the manufacturer's retail price, so please take that into account when comparing percentages off. The prices here are very good!

They will not special order any new King Hickory furniture. All of the pieces here are samples or customer cancellations.

They are not able to take credit cards, only checks or cash. Out of state checks are accepted with a driver's license. They do not ship directly to customers, but they can set up nationwide shipping for you through a third party shipper.

This is a great source! I highly recommend them!

"Athens" leather chair at the King Hickory Furniture Factory Outlet

Wholesale: $1,234.90 Discounted price: $799.00
Savings at the King Hickory Furniture Factory Outlet: $435.90 = 35% off retail

La-Z-Boy Factory Outlet

★★★★★

Manufacturer-Owned Factory Outlets, 4916 Hickory Blvd, Hickory, NC, 28601

Hours: Monday-Saturday 9:00-6:00, Sunday1:00-5:00
Phone: 828-496-2262
Email: None
Website: lazboy.com
Discount: 50%-75% off mfr retail
Payment: VISA, MasterCard, Personal Check
Delivery: White glove delivery

This is La-Z-boy's only true factory outlet. It's located in the Manufacturer-Owned Factory Outlets just north of Hickory, NC. It occupies a back corner of the Kincaid Factory Outlet, which is also owned by La-Z-Boy.

The selection is unfortunately very limited here. On my last visit, there were only a few dozen chairs to choose from, and no sofas in stock. If you do find the chair you're looking for here, you'll definitely get a great bargain.

You'll find a much larger selection of La-Z-Boy furniture (and better prices) at Coffey Furniture about five minutes north on Hwy. 321. For more information and directions, please see the individual listing in this book for Coffey Furniture.

This outlet also holds an after market sale twice each year in early May and early November when prices are discounted even further. Please check www.smartdecorating.com for current sale dates.

Vendor carries 1 manufacturer's lines

La-Z-Boy

Lane Factory Outlet

★★★★★

107 East Church Street, Martinsville, VA, 24112

Hours: Monday-Saturday 10:00-6:00
Phone: 276-632-2575
Email: hookeroutlet@hotmail.com
Website: fm-a.com
Discount: 65% off mfr retail
Payment: VISA, MasterCard, American Express, Discover, Personal Check
Delivery: White glove delivery

The Lane Factory Outlet in Martinsville, VA adjoins the Hooker Furniture Factory Outlet and is operated by the same staff. It's about an hour's drive north of High Point.

The majority of the stock at this outlet is new and in first-quality condition. Most pieces are 65% off retail. Unlike most factory outlets, this one will take phone orders. If there is a certain item you want from Lane, just call the outlet to see if they have one in stock. If they do, they'll be happy to take your order over the phone and ship it.

If you plan to visit High Point, you may wish to take a day to drive to the Martinsville, VA area, which has outlets for Hooker, Pulaski, Lane, Stanley, and Bassett, as well as a great clearance center (Martin Plaza). The bargains here are well worth the extra travel time.

Vendor carries 1 manufacturer's lines

Lane

Leather & More (Hickory) ★★★★

Hickory Furniture Mart - U. S. Hwy 70 SE, Level 4, Hickory, NC, 28602

Hours: Monday-Saturday 9:00-6:00
Phone: 828-324-0668 / 877-883-6673
Email: leatherandmore@earthlink.net
Website: leatherandmoreinhickory.com
Discount: 20%-25% off mfr retail
Payment: VISA, MasterCard, American Express, Discover, Personal Check
Delivery: White glove delivery

Leather & More has good deals on leather furniture, especially large sectionals.

On a recent visit, I found a great deal on a new special order leather sectional sofa from Omnia Leather, pictured on the following page. This "Espasio" sectional retails for $4,699.00, but you could order it through Leather & More for only $3,749.00. That's a savings of about 20% off retail. At this price, you may special order a new sofa in any color or leather style you wish.

Please bear in mind that Omnia tends to be a better value for money than many of its competitors. $3,749.00 is an excellent price for a high quality leather sectional sofa like this one. As always, please compare actual prices among competing manufacturers and discounters, not just the percentage off.

Leather & More has excellent deals on market samples in November and May after the wholesale markets in High Point. If you are shopping for leather furniture in Hickory, this store is a "must-visit".

Vendor carries 8 manufacturer's lines

Coja Leatherline	Elite Leather	Southern Lights
Collezione Divani	Legacy Leather	Zocalo
Distinctive Designs	Omnia Leather	

Omnia "Espasio" sectional sofa at Leather & More

Retail: $4,699.00 Discounted price: $3,749.00
Savings at Leather & More: $950.00 = 20% off

Lexington Factory Outlet

★★★★★

111 S Main St., Lexington, NC, 27292

Hours: Tuesday-Friday 10:00-5:00,
Saturday 9:00-4:00
Phone: 336-243-6289
Email: None
Website: None
Discount: 60% to 75% off mfr retail
Payment: VISA, MasterCard, Discover,
Personal Check
Delivery: White glove delivery

This is the only factory direct factory outlet for Lexington Home Brands, which includes the brands Lexington, Sligh, Henry Link, Aquarius, and Tommy Bahama. They have a great selection of furniture in new first-quality condition. Prices range from 60% to 75% off retail.

On a recent visit, I found a great deal on a "Mariana" display cabinet in new first-quality condition from Tommy Bahama's "Island Estate" collection (pictured on the next page). This cabinet retails for $4,500.00, but you could buy this one at the factory outlet for only $1,299.00. That's a savings of $3,201.00, or 71% off retail! It had no flaws I could find.

This is a fabulous source for beautiful upholstery and case goods at very good prices. Lexington is only about a half hour's drive from High Point, NC, and about a mile from Transit Damage Freight, which is a very good furniture source as well.

I highly recommend this factory outlet! Any furniture shopping visit to High Point should include an afternoon in Lexington to take advantage of the great deals here!

Vendor carries 5 manufacturer's lines

Aquarius Mirrorworks	Lexington	Tommy Bahama
Henry Link	Sligh	

"Mariana" display cabinet at the Lexington Factory Outlet

Retail: $4,500.00 Discounted price: $1,299.00
Savings at the Lexington Factory Outlet: $3,201.00 = 71% off retail

Lindy's Furniture (Connelly Springs) ★★★

6527 Main Circle, Connelly Springs, NC, 28612

Hours: Monday-Tuesday 9:00-5:00, Thursday-Friday 9:00-5:00, Saturday 9:00-3:00
Phone: 828-879-3000
Email: sales@lindysfurniture.com
Website: lindysfurniture.com
Discount: Up to 70% off mfr retail
Payment: VISA, MasterCard, Discover, Personal Check
Delivery: White glove delivery

Lindy's Furniture Co. has been discounting furniture for over 85 years. This store has an excellent reputation for customer service at both of their stores: Lindy's and Hudson Discount Furniture in downtown Hickory. I've always known the Hudson family to be honest and reputable dealers.

The store is huge. In addition to the four-story main building, there are 6 interconnected warehouses behind it filled with wall-to-wall furniture. The staff estimates that it takes one and a half hours to tour the entire facility straight through.

They do occasionally have floor samples, seconds, and market samples available for sale below wholesale prices. They will also sell any item off the floor, which can help you avoid shipping delays. Their special order prices are among the best.

Lindy's Furniture has an A+ record with the BBB, with only two resolved complaints during the last three years. There are no complaints at all within the last twelve months.

The store has recently begun accepting credit cards, however they do charge a 3% fee. This only covers the fee charged by the bank to offer the convenience of using a credit card. Most stores raise their prices across the board to cover the cost of using credit cards, no matter what payment method the customer actually uses, so it is good to see that only the customers using credit cards are being required to cover the additional costs charged by the bank.

They carry hundreds of lines, far more than their published list. They also promise to meet or beat any competitor's written price quote, so hold them to it! Any customer who plans to order their furniture over the phone would do well to call this source and compare their prices.

Vendor carries 86 manufacturer's lines

A.A. Importing Company	Hampton Hall	Master Design
Aico (Michael Amini)	Harden	Med Lift
American Drew	Hellenic Rugs	Miresco Rugs
Ashley Furniture	Hickory Heritage	Ohio Table Pad
Bassett Mirror	Hickory Springs	Parker House
Berkline	Hillsdale Barstools	Polrey
Bermex International	Hillstreet Beds	Powell
Best Home Furnishings	Holland House	Primo
Brooks	Holly Springs	Progressive Furniture
Broyhill	Hooker	Pulaski
Cambridge Chair	Howard Miller	Ridgeway Clocks
Canal Dover	Hubbardton Forge	Riverside Furniture
Catnapper	Imperial Bedding	Rowe Furniture
Chromcraft	Jackson Furniture	Sam Moore
Clayton Marcus	Jamison	Schnadig
Coaster Fine Furniture	Jimson	Shadow Mountain
Cochrane Furniture	Joffran	South Sea Rattan
Craftique	Kincaid	Tennessee Enterprises
Cramco	King Hickory	Tradewinds
Crawford of Jamestown	Kingsdown	Trans-Ocean Import Co
Davis International	La-Z-Boy	Troutman Chair
Decor Rest	Lane	Two Day Designs
Elliotts Designs	Lea Industries	Universal Furniture
England Corsair	Legacy Leather	Uwharrie Chair
Fairfax	Lexington	Vaughan Bassett
Fairfield Chair	Liberty	Vaughan Furniture
Fashion Bed Group	Ligo Products	Winners Only
Gotico	Luke Leather	Wynwood
Hammary	Magnussen Home	

Lindy's Furniture (Hickory)

★★★★

233 1st Ave NW, Hickory, NC, 28601

Hours: Monday-Tuesday 9:00-5:30, Thursday-Friday 9:00-5:30, Saturday 9:00-3:00
Phone: 828-327-8986
Email: sales@lindysfurniture.com
Website: lindysfurniture.com
Discount: Up to 70% off mfr retail
Payment: VISA, MasterCard, Personal Check
Delivery: White glove delivery

Lindys Furniture in downtown Hickory, NC (formerly known as Hudson Discount Furniture) has been discounting furniture for over 83 years. They have an excellent reputation. It's owned by the same family that owns and operates Lindy's Furniture in Connelly Springs.

Lindy's Furniture has an A+ record with the BBB, with only two resolved complaints during the last three years across all three of their stores. There are no complaints at all within the last twelve months.

The store has recently begun accepting credit cards, however they do charge a 3% fee. This only covers the fee charged by the bank to offer the convenience of using a credit card. Most stores raise their prices across the board to cover the cost of using credit cards, no matter what payment method the customer actually uses, so it is good to see that only the customers using credit cards are being required to cover the additional costs charged by the bank.

They are very reputable and pleasant to work with. I highly recommend this source!

Vendor carries 88 manufacturer's lines

A.A. Importing Company
Aico (Michael Amini)
American Drew
Amindo Furniture
Ashley Furniture
Bassett Mirror
Benchcraft
Berkline
Bermex International
Best Chair
Brooks
Broyhill
Cambridge Chair
Canal Dover
Catnapper
Chromcraft
Clayton Marcus
Coaster Fine Furniture
Cochrane Furniture
Craftique
Cramco
Crawford of Jamestown
Davis International
Decor Rest
Elliotts Designs
England Corsair
Fairfax
Fairfield Chair
Fashion Bed Group
Flexsteel

Gotico
Hammary
Hekman
Hellenic Rugs
Hickory Heritage
Hickory Hill
Hickory Springs
Hillsdale Barstools
Hillstreet Beds
Holland House
Holly Springs
Hooker
Howard Miller
Hubbardton Forge
Imperial Bedding
Jackson Furniture
Jamison
Jimson
Joffran
Kincaid
King Hickory
Kingsdown
La-Z-Boy
Lane
Lea Industries
Legacy Classic
Lexington
Liberty
Ligo Products
Luke Leather

Magnussen Home
Master Design
Med Lift
Miresco Rugs
Ohio Table Pad
Parker House
Polrey
Powell
Primo
Pulaski
Ridgeway Clocks
Riverside Furniture
Rowe Furniture
Sam Moore
Schnadig
South Sea Rattan
Sumter Cabinet
Tennessee Enterprises
Tradewinds
Trans-Ocean Import Co
Troutman Chair
Two's Company
Universal Furniture
Uwharrie Chair
Vaughan Bassett
Vaughan Furniture
Winners Only
Wynwood

Mackie Furniture Co

13 N. Main St., Granite Falls, NC, 28630

Hours: Monday-Tuesday 8:30-5:30, Wednesday 8:30-3:00, Thursday-Friday 8:30-5:30, Saturday 8:30-3:00
Phone: 828-396-3313
Email: info@mackiefurniture.com
Website: mackiefurniture.com
Discount: 40%-50% off mfr retail
Payment: VISA, MasterCard, Personal Check
Delivery: White glove delivery

Mackie Furniture Co. is just a few miles north of Hickory, NC. The store has showrooms on two floors, with a nice variety of medium quality furniture from brands like Bassett, Lane, Universal, Pulaski, and Ashley.

On a recent visit, I found a great deal on Lane reclining furniture. The #402 "Grayson" leather rocker recliner pictured on the next page retails for $799.00, but this chair at Mackie Furniture was marked down to $439.00. That's a savings of $360.00, or 45% off retail. It was in new, first-quality condition.

Mackie Furniture has had a spotless record with the BBB for many years. I've never heard a single complaint about them. I highly recommend this source!

Vendor carries 31 manufacturer's lines

Action by Lane	Fairfield Chair	McKay Table Pads
American Drew	Fashion Bed Group	Philip Reinisch
Ashley Furniture	Heather Brooke	Powell
Bassett	Hooker	Pulaski
Bob Mackie	Jessica McClintock	Riverside Furniture
Broyhill	Keller	Telescope
Carolina Mattress	Kincaid	Timmerman
Carolina Mirror	Kingsdown	Universal Furniture
Clayton Marcus	Lane	Vaughan Furniture
Cochrane Furniture	Lea Industries	
Eddie Bauer by Lane	Lloyd/Flanders	

Lane rocker recliner at Mackie Furniture Co.

Retail: $799.00 Discounted price: $439.00
Savings at Mackie Furniture Co.: $360.00 = 45% off retail

Maitland-Smith Factory Outlet ★★★★★

Hickory Furniture Mart - U. S. Hwy 70 SE, Level 1, Hickory, NC, 28602

Hours: Monday-Saturday 9:00-6:00
Phone: 828-322-7111
Email: hfosales@henredonoutlet.com
Website: maitland-smith.com
Discount: 50%-75% off mfr retail
Payment: VISA, MasterCard, American Express, Discover, Personal Check
Delivery: White glove delivery

The factory outlet for Maitland-Smith and LaBarge in High Point has moved to the Hickory Furniture Mart. Hickory Outlet Center at the Hickory Furniture Mart also carries some pieces from Maitland-Smith. There are no other factory authorized sources for Maitland-Smith outlet furniture.

The Maitland-Smith factory outlet has combined sales and shipping with its sister store, the Henredon Factory Outlet, right next door at the Hickory Furniture Mart.

Most of the pieces here are floor samples and discontinued items, although there are a few seconds. Even the seconds have extremely small flaws, however. The discounts are very good: 60%-70% off retail.

On a recent visit, I found a deal on a discontinued "Bowmont" dining room set by Maitland-Smith in new first-quality condition. The table and 6 chairs retail for $28,995.00, but the regular outlet price was only $10,443.00. That's a savings of $18,552.00, or 64% off retail. The outlet set had no damage or flaws I could find.

Plus, during the after market sale when I took this photo, the Maitland-Smith factory outlet was offering an extra 25% off of their regular outlet prices. That brought the price of this set down an additional $2,611.00, for a total savings of $21,163.00, or 73% off of the regular retail price!

The outlet will not special order new Maitland-Smith furniture, but if you see a Maitland-Smith piece you like at a local furniture store, you can call the outlet to see if they might have a floor sample or a similar discontinued style. The outlet will take these types of orders by phone and have your furniture shipped to you.

"Bowmont" dining room set from Maitland Smith

Retail: $28,995.00 Discounted price: $7,832.00
Savings at the Maitland Smith Factory Outlet: $21,163.00 = 73% off retail

Vendor carries 2 manufacturer's lines

La Barge   Maitland-Smith

Martin Plaza

★★★★★

115 East Church Street, Martinsville, VA, 24112

Hours: Monday-Saturday 10:00-6:00
Phone: 276-638-2040
Email: showroom@fm-a.com
Website: fm-a.com
Discount: 50%-60% off mfr retail
Payment: VISA, MasterCard, American Express, Discover, Personal Check
Delivery: White glove delivery

Martin Plaza in Martinsville, VA is the clearance center for The Showroom, owned by Fred Martin Associate. FMA also owns factory outlets for Hooker, Bassett, Lane, and Darlee Outdoor Furniture on the same street.

They have a great reputation for service, and the staff is very helpful. Martinsville is about an hour's drive north of High Point. The most of the stock at this outlet are floor samples and discontinued items in very good condition. A few pieces may have slight flaws, but I didn't see any flawed pieces on my last visit. Most pieces are 50%-60% off retail.

For instance, on a recent visit I found a great deal on a "Venice" china hutch from Century (pictured on the following page. This hutch normally retails for $4,706.00, but you could buy this one on clearance for only $2,369.00, a savings of 50% off retail. This floor sample had no flaws I could find.

They may have pieces from any line sold by The Showroom, but the majority of the stock here is from Century, Hooker, and Lane.

Unlike most factory outlets and clearance centers, this one will take phone orders. If there is a certain item you want, just call the clearance center to see if they have one in stock.

All of the furniture discounters and factory outlets owned by the Martin family have had spotless records with the BBB for many years with no complaints whatsoever. I've always been very pleased with how they've worked with my private clients and shopping tours.

If you plan to visit High Point, you may wish to take a day to drive to the Martinsville, VA area, which also has outlets for Hooker, Lane, Pulaski, Stanley, and Bassett. The bargains here are well worth the extra travel time.

Century hutch at Martin Plaza

Retail: $4,706.00 Discounted price: $2,369.00
Savings at Martin Plaza: $2,337.00 = 50% off retail

Vendor carries 20 manufacturer's lines

Action by Lane	Hooker	Stanley
American Drew	Kessler	Sumter Cabinet
APA Marketing	King Hickory	Taylor King
Butler Specialty	Lane	Ultimate Accents
Century Furniture	LeatherTrend	Woodmark Furniture
Fairfield Chair	Passport	Wynwood
Hekman	Sarreid	

Merinos (Jefferson, GA) ★

28 Epps St., Jefferson, GA, 30549

Hours: Monday-Saturday 10:00-6:00, Sunday1:00-5:00
Phone: 706-387-0065
Email: merinosusa@aol.com
Website: merinosfurniture.com
Discount: 50% to 55% off mfr retail
Payment: VISA, MasterCard, American Express, Discover, Personal Check
Delivery: Local delivery only

Merinos Home Furnishings in Jefferson, GA is huge! All three Merinos stores in Georgia, North Carolina, and South Carolina are located in former mill buildings. This means they are huge, no-frills, and way off the beaten path. Jefferson, GA is about an hour north of Atlanta.

Is it worth the drive? Not really. The furniture here is all from medium quality brands like Lane, Powell, Best, etc. The discounts are not marked on the tags, but we can do some comparisons with other sources that don't require such a long drive.

For instance, on a recent visit, I found the England "Monroe" loveseat (stock #1436) pictured on the next page. Merinos' price on this loveseat was $635.00 in stock. Other online sources list the same loveseat for lower prices, including Furniture Liquidators which sells the identical loveseat for $559.00. That's not a bargain.

Merinos carries low to medium end brands readily available in any metropolitan area for similar prices. Occasionally, I have found discounts here of up to 20% off comparable stores, but most of the furniture here is priced about the same as at any low-end discount furniture store nationwide. There's nothing special here in style or price, and definitely nothing to justify driving so far out of town.

I had to laugh at their web site. The "construction" link in the left menu at the bottom of their main web page takes you to photos of construction of the building. Really? Any other furniture website would be giving information on the construction of the furniture.

147

England Sofa at Merinos

Merinos price: 635.00 Furniture Liquidators price: $559.00
Savings at Merinos: none

Vendor carries 32 manufacturer's lines

A R T Furniture
A-America
Acme Metal Products
American Drew
Ashley Furniture
Bernhardt
Best Home Furnishings
Bradington Young
Brooks
Broughton Hall
Broyhill

England Corsair
Futura Leather
Hammary
Homelegance
Hooker
Kincaid
Lane
Largo
Lea Industries
Leather Italia USA
Magnussen Home

Millennium
Orient Express Furniture
Powell
Pulaski
Sam Moore
Schnadig
Signature Designs
Thomasville
Universal Furniture
Vaughan Bassett

Merinos (Mooresville, NC)   ★

500 S. Main St., Mooresville, NC, 28115

Hours: Monday-Saturday 10:00-6:00, Sunday1:00-5:00
Phone: 704-660-0445
Email: merinosusa@aol.com
Website: merinosfurniture.com
Discount: 50-55% off retail
Payment: VISA, MasterCard, American Express, Discover, Personal Check
Delivery: Local delivery only

Merinos Home Furnishings in Mooresville, NC is closer to civilization than their other locations. Mooresville is roughly between Hickory and High Point, but not very convenient to either.

Is it worth making a side trip to Merinos during your Hickory or High Point shopping trip? Not really. They carry low to medium end brands readily available in any metropolitan area for similar prices. Occasionally, I have found discounts here of up to 20% off comparable stores, but most of the furniture here is priced about the same as at any low-end discount furniture store nationwide. There's nothing special here in style or price, and definitely nothing to justify taking a half day out of your trip to Hickory or High Point.

Here's the best bargain I found at Merinos in Mooresville during my most recent visit. This is the "Osmond" living room set by Best Home Furnishings (pictured on the following page). The sofa pictured retails for 1,599.00, but you can buy this one at Merino's for $821.44. The loveseat retails for $1,620.00, but you could buy this loveseat at Merinos for $848.69. The chair retails for $1,479.00, but you can buy it at Merinos for $678.30. The complete set sells for $2,348.43. This price does not include shipping. Merinos only delivers locally, but they can arrange shipping nationwide for a higher fee.

You can also order the identical set at www.cabelas.com for $2,799.97 with free curbside delivery nationwide. Costs to have the same set shipped from Merinos to your home will vary depending on where you live, but the shoppers in the vast majority of states will surely find that it costs more than $451.54 to have this set shipped from Merinos to their house.

149

Sofa by Best Home Furnishings at Merinos

Merinos price: 2,348.43.00 (no ship) Cabelas.com price: $2,799.97.00 (free ship)

Savings at Merinos: $451.54 or 16% off competitor's price if customer picks up at Merinos. Other customers will pay extra for shipping.

Vendor carries 33 manufacturer's lines

A R T Furniture	England Corsair	Millennium
A-America	Futura Leather	Orient Express Furniture
Acme Metal Products	Hammary	Powell
American Drew	Homelegance	Pulaski
Ashley Furniture	Hooker	Sam Moore
Bernhardt	Kincaid	Schnadig
Best Home Furnishings	Lane	Shaw Flooring
Bradington Young	Largo	Signature Designs
Brooks	Lea Industries	Thomasville
Broughton Hall	Leather Italia USA	Universal Furniture
Broyhill	Magnussen Home	Vaughan Bassett

Mitchell Gold Factory Outlet ★★★

Hickory Furniture Mart - U. S. Hwy 70 SE, Level 1, Hickory, NC, 28602

Hours: Monday-Saturday 9:00-6:00
Phone: (828) 261-0051
Email: mgbwoutlet@hotmail.com
Website: mitchellgold.com
Discount: About 50% off mfr retail
Payment: VISA, MasterCard, Personal Check
Delivery: White glove delivery

Mitchell Gold + Bob Williams make a well-known line of upholstered and slipcovered furniture under their own names, as well as for Pottery Barn, Restoration Hardware, and Williams Sonoma. You will usually find items from all of these brands at the Hickory Furniture Mart outlet.

All of the upholstered furniture here is American made, at their nearby factory in Taylorsville, NC. The case goods are imported.

Discounts here run 50% off the manufacturers suggested retail price. For example, I found a sectional group from the "Stephon" collection for only $1,773.00 for both pieces (pictured on the following page). The retail price I put under the picture is estimated, based on statements by the staff at this outlet that the furniture here is priced at 50% off retail.

They will not special order any pieces. You must choose from what is in stock. Many items are just single pieces, but there are some sets in stock. Most of the furniture I saw on my visit was in new or almost new condition. The outlet sells overstock items, discontinued collections, showroom samples, and retailer returns.

Compared to the Mitchell Gold retail stores, Pottery Barn, etc, the furniture here is a great deal. Compared to competitors like Club Furniture, the Century Furniture factory outlet, and other companies that sell upholstered furniture factory direct to the public, the Mitchell Gold outlet is not such a great deal.

For example, Club Furniture offers a sectional that is very similar to the one I photographed for this book (their Cosmopolitan Contemporary Sectional), and you can buy the Club Furniture sectional new in any color they offer for only about $160.00 more than Mitchell Gold is charging for this one set in the outlet where you have to take just the color and configuration they happen to have in stock when you visit.

To be fair, the sectionals are not completely identical. The Mitchell Gold sectional has more tufting in the cushions, but the Club Furniture set offers bolsters where the Mitchell Gold sectional did not. I find them comparable. The construction details are almost identical, and they are certainly of comparable quality.

Sectional sofa from Mitchell Gold + Bob Williams

Retail (estimated): $3,546.00 Discounted price: $1,773.00
Savings at the Mitchell Gold Factory Outlet: $1,773.00 = 50% off retail

Priba Furniture Sales and Interiors ★★★★

210 Stage Coach Trail, Greensboro, NC, 27415

Hours: Monday-Friday 9:00-5:30, Saturday 9:00-5:00
Phone: 336-855-9034
Email: info@pribafurniture.com
Website: pribafurniture.com
Discount: 35%-50% off mfr retail
Payment: VISA, MasterCard, Personal Check
Delivery: White glove delivery

Priba Furniture Sales and Interiors is located in Greensboro, NC, just north of High Point. They have a good selection of medium to high-end lines, including Craftique, Century, and Baker. You will find some of the best brands available on the market here. Discounts run from 50%-60% off retail. They have some of the best bargains I've seen on high-end brands.

On a recent visit, I found a great deal on a beautiful painted Chinoiserie chest by Sarreid (pictured on the next page). This chest retails for $2,445.00, but you can order a new one from Priba for $1,223.00. That's a savings of $1,222.00, or 50% off retail! This chest is very typical of the high-end luxurious furniture you will find at this store. Their selection is definitely a cut above most of their North Carolina competitors.

They have some great deals for out of state shoppers, too. Priba offers a 1% rebate toward the cost of one night's hotel bill if you visit their store and make a purchase.

Priba has an excellent record of customer service going back over 35 years. As of this writing in February 2016 they have an A+ rating with the BBB.

If you're planning to order your furniture by phone, especially high end brands, definitely give this source a call to compare their prices.

153

Sarreid chest at Priba Furniture

Retail: $2,445.00 Discounted price: $1,223.00
Savings at Priba Furniture: $1,222.00 = 50% off retail

Vendor carries 200 manufacturer's lines

A R T Furniture	Better Homes	Charleston Forge
A. A. Laun	Bolier	Chatham Crossing
Abner Henry	Borkholder	Chelsea House
Accents Beyond	Boston Rockers	Chromcraft
Action by Lane	Bradington Young	Classic Elements
Adagio	Bramble Company	Classic Gallery
Adams Furniture	Braxton Culler	Classic Leather
Ambella Home	British Traditions	Cochrane Furniture
American Drew	Brown Jordan	Colonial Furniture
American Woodcrafters	Brown Street	Conover Chair
Ardley Hall	Butler Specialty	Councill
Art For Kids	C. R. Laine Upholstery	Cox Manufacturing Co
Artistica Metal Designs	Canadel	Craftique
Baker Furniture	Cape Craftsmen	Crawford of Jamestown
Barcalounger	Carolina Tables	Creative Metal & Wood
Bassett Mirror	Carter Furniture	Cresent

Bernard Christianson
Bernhardt
David Michael
Davis Cabinets
Decorative Crafts
Designmaster
Dinec
Distinction Leather
Drexel Heritage
Dutailier
Elliotts Designs
Elysee Collection
EXL Designs Upholstery
Fairfield Chair
Fashion Bed Group
Fauld
Ficks Reed
Fjords
Flat Rock Furniture
Fremarc Designs
French Heritage
Gat Creek
Glass Arts
Gloster
Gotico
Grande Arredo
Guildmaster
Hancock & Moore
Heather Brooke
Henkel Harris
Hickory Chair
High Point Furniture
Hillsdale Barstools
Holland House
Hooker
Howard Miller
Hunt Country Furniture
J. D. Young and Sons
Jasper Cabinet
Jessica Charles
John-Richard
Johnston Casuals

Cebu Furniture
Century Furniture
Lea Industries
Leathercraft
Lee Industries
Legacy Classic
Linwood
Lloyd/Flanders
Louis J. Solomon
Luke Leather
MacKenzie Dow
Magnussen Home
Maitland-Smith
Massoud Furniture
McGuire
McKay Table Pads
McKinley Leather
Michael Thomas
Miles Talbott
Mobel
Modern History
Moosehead
Morgan Hill
Motioncraft
Newport Cabinet
Norwalk Furniture
Oak Designs
Ohio Table Pad
Old Hickory Tannery
Opus Designs
Our House Designs
P & P Chair
Palatial Leather
Palecek
PAMA
Pastel
Paula Deen Home
Payne Street Imports
Pearson
Peters-Revington
Polywood
Port Eliot

CTH Sherrill Occasional
David Lee Design
Sam Moore
Sarreid
Scheibeco
Schnadig
Seabrook Wallcovering
Serta
Seven Seas Seating
Shermag
Sherrill
Sligh
Somerset
Southampton
Southern Furniture
Southwood
Spring Air
St. Timothy
Stanford
Statesville Chair
Stein World
Stone County Ironworks
Style Upholstery
Superior Furniture
Taylorsville
Thayer Coggin
The Custom Shoppe
Theodore Alexander
Thomasville
Three Coins
Tom Seely Furniture
Trade Winds Furniture
Tropitone
Trosby Furniture
Troutman Chair
Universal Furniture
Uwharrie Chair
Vaughan Bassett
Venture By Lane
Vermont Tubbs
Wesley Allen
Wesley Hall

Karges
Keystone Collections
Kincaid
Kindel
King Hickory
Kittinger
La Barge
Lane
Laneventure

Precedent
Pulaski
Randall-Allan
Rare Collections
Riverside Furniture
Robert & Robert
Robert Allen Fabrics
Robin Bruce
Rowe Furniture

Whitecraft Rattan
Winston
Woodard Furniture
Woodbridge
Woodmark Furniture
World Design Center
Wright Table
Yorkshire House

Reflections ★★★★★

Hickory Furniture Mart - U. S. Hwy. 70 SE, Hickory, NC, 28602

Hours: Monday-Saturday 9:00-6:00
Phone: 828-327-8485
Email: See Web site
Website: reflectionsfurniture.com
Discount: 40%-50% off mfr retail
Payment: VISA, MasterCard, American Express, Discover, Personal Check
Delivery: White glove delivery

Reflections has a great selection of contemporary furniture, which can be in short supply in North Carolina. They have a nice Natuzzi gallery, plus they carry a wide variety of other unique lines, listed below. Ekornes, in particular, has a very nice line of contemporary motion furniture. Prices tend to run 40%-50% off retail.

On my most recent visit, I found a great deal on Lazar's popular Corkscrew Swivel Chair with Crescent Ottoman (pictured on the next page). The chair retails for $1,199.00, but you can get this one at Reflections for $748.00. That's a savings of $451.00, or 38% off retail!

The matching Crescent Ottoman isn't available at retailers, but you can buy this one at Reflections for $348.00.

Reflections typically offers extra discounts of 10% off special order furniture during the Mart-wide sales and after-market sales.

Bargains on contemporary furniture are hard to come by, even in North Carolina. If you're looking for contemporary styles, you will find some of the best bargains here.

Reflections has been discounting contemporary furniture in North Carolina for over thirty years. The BBB also gives them an A+ rating without a single complaint on record. I've never received any reader complaints about them either. I highly recommend this source!

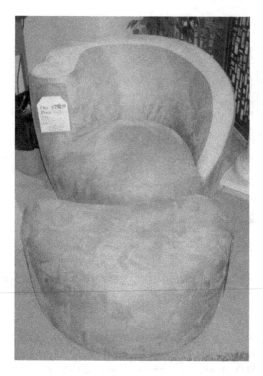

Lazar Corkscrew chair from Reflections

Retail price: $1,199.00 Discounted price: $748.00
Savings at Reflections: $451.00 = 38% off retail

Vendor carries 25 manufacturer's lines

American Leather	Ekornes	Natuzzi
Amisco	Foreign Accents	Oriental Weavers
Artisan House, inc	Gamma	Progressive Furniture
Artists Guild of America	George Kovacs Lighting	Star
BDI/Becker Designed	Johnston Casuals	Stone International
Calligaris	Jozefina	Trica
Creative Elegance	Kalalou	Van Teal
Decorize	Lazar Industries	
Dream Weavers	Ligna	

Simplicity Sofas

2726 English Rd, High Point, NC

Hours: Monday-Friday 9:00-6:00
Phone: 336-882-2490 / 800-813-2889
Email: Please see Web site
Website: simplicitysofas.com
Discount: Factory direct to the public
Payment: VISA, MasterCard, American Express, Discover, Personal Check
Delivery: Furniture is delivered boxed and ready to assemble via UPS or FEDEX Ground.

Simplicity Sofas in High Point, NC offers a wide range of upholstered furniture: full size sofas, sectionals, chairs, and sleeper sofas.

Their patented assembly system and factory direct sales allow Simplicity Sofas to offer a wide variety of popular upholstery styles at about 10%-20% less than similar items from their competitors built to the same level of quality.

It is good quality furniture for the price. All frames are solid oak, and they use sinuous springs (like Mitchell Gold, Pottery Barn, Restoration Hardware, La-Z-Boy, Broyhill, Club Furniture, and comparable brands). Cushions can be ordered in two options: 8" Ultracel foam wrapped in dacron (firm) or 8" spring-down construction (plush). All cushions have zip off covers for cleaning.

You can request fabric swatches, or supply your own fabric through their COM program. "COM" refers to "Customers Own Material". You can also request a sleeper sofa upgrade on any sofa they make for an additional $195.00, which is a good deal for a sleeper sofa.

You can also purchase slipcovers for any piece, which is convenient if you have young children or pets. The slipcovers are very nice looking fitted slipcovers custom tailored for each piece, not the one-size-fits-all tents you find at linens stores. They look good.

Please note that this furniture will arrive boxed and ready to assemble. Assembly is simple and typically does not take longer than 15-30 minutes per piece. Full instructions are given at the web site.

This site offers a good product for locations where doors are narrow and spaces are tight, such as in recreational vehicles, boats, or older apartments.

Simplicity Sofas has a spotless record with the BBB. I've never heard a single complaint about them. They offer no questions asked returns for one year after purchase (with the exception of furniture special ordered in the customer's own fabric), and all freight is refunded -- both ways. This is the most generous return policy I've seen from any furniture source. I am also very impressed that their customer service department calls every customer within one business day of delivery to ask if the consumer has any questions or concerns about their delivery.

If you are in the High Point area looking for this type of furniture, you should definitely stop in. They often have floor samples available at 50% off the prices at their web site.

Sobol House Of Furnishings   ★

141 Richardson Blvd., Black Mountain, NC, 28711

Hours: Monday-Saturday 9:30-5:00
Phone: 828-669-8031
Email: sales@sobolhouse.com
Website: sobolhouse.com
Discount: 40%-60% off mfr retail
Payment: VISA, MasterCard, Personal Check
Delivery: White glove delivery

Sobol House Of Furnishings is located in Black Mountain, NC, just east of Asheville. They offer a good selection of medium to high-end lines by phone order, including Bevan-Funnell, Flexsteel, Barcalounger, and Braxton Culler.

The store is filled with cheap, randomly placed furniture. The only salesperson on duty when I visited was the owner, Woody Sobol. I visited the store on a Saturday in early November, which is one of the two biggest sales periods in North Carolina. Other stores nearby had plenty of customers, but not this one.

Overall, Sobol House does not present itself as a professional business. I can't recommend shopping here. Tyson Furniture in Black Mountain is a much better place to shop if you are in this area. All of the brands carried by Sobol House can also be ordered at the same (or better) prices from competing discounters with better records of customer service. Please use the brand index in this book to find them.

Vendor carries 80 manufacturer's lines

A.P. Generations	Bassett	Cambridge Chair
A.P. Industries	Bassett Mirror	Capel Rugs
American Drew	Basta Sole by Tropitone	Capris Furniture
Arte de Mexico	Berkline	Carolina Mirror
Athol Tables	Bevan-Funnell	Century Furniture
Barcalounger	Braxton Culler	Cochrane Furniture
Bard International	Builtright Chair	Colibri Furniture

Colonial Furniture	Karges	Southern Craftsmen
Conover Chair	Kessler	Stakmore
Cooper Classics	Key City Furniture	Stein World
Craftique	King Hickory	Superior Furniture
Davis Cabinets	Kushwood	Taylor King
Decorative Crafts	Lea Industries	TeenaIron Works
Designz Unlimited	Legacy Classic	Three Coins
Destinations	Lloyd Buxton	Timmerman
Eddy West	Miller Desk	Universal Furniture
Environment	Old Biscayne Designs	Vaughan Furniture
Fairfield Chair	Old Hickory Furniture	Vietri
Fairmont Designs	Ozark Cedar	Waterford Crystal
Flat Rock Furniture	Passport	Weiman
Flexsteel	Pompeii	Wesley Allen
Hammary	Pulaski	Wesley Hall
Hammerton	Reprocrafters	Whitaker Furniture
Hickory Springs	Riverside Furniture	Wildwood Lamps
Homecrest	Sarreid	Wynwood
Howard Miller	Scheibeco	Yorkshire House
Johnston Casuals	Serta	

Southern Style

★★★★★

Hickory Furniture Mart - U. S. Hwy. 70 SE, Level 4, Hickory, NC, 28602

Hours: Monday-Saturday 9:00-6:00
Phone: 828-322-7000
Email: sales@ssfinefurniture.com
Website: southernstylefinefurniture.com
Discount: 40%-50% off mfr retail
Payment: VISA, MasterCard, American Express, Discover, Personal Check
Delivery: White glove delivery

Southern Style specializes in upholstery by Southern Furniture of Conover. They've also got a number of high quality wicker and casegoods lines, listed below. Their discounts run 40%-50% off retail.

For instance, on a recent visit I found a good deal on a nice group from Southern Furniture (pictured on the following page). This loveseat retails for $2,600.00, and the chair retails for $1,629.00. You could special order these items through Southern Style for $1,379.00 for the loveseat and $869.00 for the chair, a total discount of 47% off retail.

They will sell most items off the floor. These floor samples are generally not marked down on the tags, but I've found that you can still negotiate a discount on most items if you try.

If you're interested in any of the lines below, this store is well worth checking out. They have a very good reputation for customer service, and a spotless record with the BBB. I've never heard a complaint about them.

Loveseat and chair at Southern Style

Retail: $4,229.00 Discounted price: $2,248.00
Savings at Southern Style: $1,981.00 = 47% off retail

Vendor carries 26 manufacturer's lines

APA Marketing	Castilian Imports	Magnussen Home
Ayca	D & F Wicker Rattan	Restonic
Bailey Street	Eddy West	Southern Furniture
Bentley Churchill	Emerson et Cie	Stein World
Bernard Molyneux Coll	FFDM	Ultimate Accents
Best Chair	Habersham	Viewpoint
Boca Rattan	John-Richard	World Concepts
Braxton Culler	Lorts	Wynwood
Carrington Court	Luna Bella	

Stanley Furniture Factory Outlet ★★

20100 Virgil H Goode Highway, Rocky Mount, VA, 24151

Hours: Monday-Friday 9:00-6:00,
Saturday 10:00-5:00, Sunday1:00-5:00
Phone: 540-489-8000
Email: None
Website: stanleyfurniture.com
Discount: 60% off retail
Payment: VISA, MasterCard, Discover,
Personal Check
Delivery: East Coast only

The Stanley Furniture Factory Outlet moved in late 2008 from their longtime location in Bassett, VA, to the Blue Ridge Antique Market in Rocky Mount, VA, about 20 miles further north on Hwy. 220. Overall, the new outlet is a disappointment, with smaller selection and higher prices than the old outlet.

Prices here run about 60% off retail across the board. Most items are in first quality condition: overstocks, discontinued pieces, showroom samples, and retailer returns. A few items have very minor damage, although they do not seem to be priced any lower than the undamaged pieces. You will find some complete sets, and many odd pieces. There is also a small selection of childrens furniture from Stanley's "Young America" line.

For example, on a recent visit, I found a vanity desk in first quality condition from their "Isabella" line (pictured on the following page) for $535.00. That is 59% off the retail price of $1,299.00. There were no matching pieces.

If you are looking for specific clearance items from Stanley Furniture, you may wish to check Furnitureland South's two clearance centers in and near High Point before you drive 90 minutes north of High Point to Rocky Mount, VA. You might find what you are looking for at prices nearly as low as the outlet. For instance, I found the very same vanity desk at Furnitureland On Main the same week for only $575.00.

Please note that this outlet will not arrange shipping at all. Your can bring a truck, or you may wish to call Hopkins Delivery Service at 276-647-5200. John Hopkins has been delivering furniture from the factory outlets in Virginia reliably for many years. They do have people on site who will help you with

165

loading. If you bring your own truck, you will need to also bring blankets and ties to wrap your purchases as most pieces are not in the original factory box.

You will also find a few outlet pieces here from other lines such as Cooper Classics, Aspen, Cresent, and Bassett Mirror, all manufactured nearby. There is a factory outlet right next door for Uttermost decorative accessories with some very good prices on wall art, vases, and other small accessories.

This source does charge Virginia sales tax whether you are having items shipped to another state or not. They also do not take phone orders under any circumstances. Please note than any purchases must be picked up by you or your freight company within 7 days.

I did not find that the price and selection at this factory outlet justified the driving time to come here, especially with the limited customer service.

"Isabella" Vanity desk from Stanley Young America

Retail: $1,299.00 Discounted price: $535.00
Savings at the Stanley Factory Outlet: $764.00 = 59% off retail

Stickley Furniture Showroom   ★

225 North Elm St., High Point, NC, 27260

Hours: Monday-Saturday 9:00-5:00
Phone: 336-887-1336
Email: None
Website: stickley.com
Discount: None. Only North Carolina residents are allowed to shop here.
Payment: VISA, MasterCard, Personal Check
Delivery: None

I don't quite understand the point of the sign that sits invitingly outside the Stickley Furniture Showroom in High Point, NC.

The sign cheerily invites us in: "Open to the Public!" Once inside, though, a woman behind an overpriced desk stiffly informs visitors, "You can look, but you can't buy anything".

What? Odd policy for a furniture store. Odd policy for any store. I don't know of anywhere else that has this policy, other than Cuba.

Alas, the woman guarding the showroom cannot be persuaded. She says I can browse around all I like, and then go back to whereever I came from and order my furniture at full price from my local Stickley dealer and wait 2 months for shipment.

Well, of course. Isn't that what all furniture buyers travel to High Point, North Carolina to do? Browse a showroom marked with wholesale discounts, and then go back home to pay full price?

Please do not waste time setting foot in this building. There are better brands than Stickley that are just as well-built, look just as good, and don't tease!

One great alternative is American Accents about 15 minutes away in Jamestown. They have furniture in the same style as Stickley from high quality Amish manufacturers, and they really do have great North Carolina prices.

Studio Rowe ★

Furniture Avenue Galleries, 4350 Furniture Ave., Jamestown, NC, 27282

Hours: Tuesday-Saturday 9:30-5:30
Phone: 336-885-8300
Email: None
Website: kagansfurnitureonline.com
Discount: 30%-50% off mfr retail
Payment: Personal Check
Delivery: White glove delivery

Studio Rowe at the Furniture Avenue Galleries in Jamestown, NC, is a subsidiary of Kagan's Furniture. Owner Ike Kagan purchased the mall building in 2009. He owns all the galleries inside except for American Accents and Decorator's Choice.

They have a nice selection of Rowe upholstery at 30%-60% off retail. For example, on a recent visit I found this "Laine" chair by Rowe Furniture (pictured on the next page).

The manufacturer's retail on this chair is $1,039.99, but you could buy this one off the floor at Studio Rowe for $495. That's a savings of $544.99, or 52% off retail. The chair appeared to be in new, first-quality condition. Shipping costs extra.

"Laine" chair by Rowe Furniture at Studio Rowe

Retail: $1,039.99 Discounted price: $495.00
Savings at Studio Rowe: $544.99 = 52% off retail

Vendor carries 1 manufacturer's lines

Rowe Furniture

Tarheel Furniture ★★

3351 Hickory Blvd., Hudson, NC, 28638

Hours: Monday-Saturday 9:00-6:00
Phone: 828-396-1942
Email: sales@furnitureshoppe.com
Website: furnitureshoppe.com
Discount: 40%-60% off mfr retail
Payment: VISA, MasterCard, Discover, Personal Check
Delivery: White glove delivery

Tarheel Furniture has some good bargains, particularly on Kincaid Furniture. On a recent visit, I found a great deal on a "Carriage House" dining room set by Kincaid. This set with the table, four side chairs, and two arm chairs retails for $4,140.00, but you could buy this set for only $2,419.00, a savings of $1,721.00 or 42% off the retail price.

In March 2005, the Tarheel Furniture bought out The Furniture Shoppe and moved into its former location. The web site www.tarheelhomefurnishings.com is no longer active, only www.furnitureshoppe.com. So, please note that both names currently refer to the same company.

As of this writing in March 2016 Tarheel Furniture has an A+ rating with the BBB.

Kincaid "Carriage House" dining room set at Tarheel Furniture

Retail: $4,140.00 Discounted price: $2,419.00
Savings at Tarheel Furniture: $1,721.00 = 42% off retail

Vendor carries 61 manufacturer's lines

American Drew
Bassett
Bassett Baby/Juvenile
Bassett Mirror
Best Chair
Braxton Culler
Butler Specialty
Canal Dover
Carlton McLendon
Carolina Mirror
Christopher Lowell
Chromcraft
Classic Leather
Clayton Marcus
Craftique
D. R. Kincaid
Dalyn Rug Company
Dinaire
Dutailier
Fairfield Chair
Flexsteel

Furniture Designs/Choice
Hammary
Homelegance
Hooker
Interlude
Jessica McClintock
Joffran
Johnston Casuals
Kincaid
Laneventure
Lea Industries
Legacy Classic
Magnussen Home
Master Design
Mobel
Ohio Table Pad
Overnight Sofas
Palliser
Peopleloungers
Peters-Revington
Philip Reinisch

Powell
Pulaski
Riverside Furniture
Rowe Furniture
Sam Moore
Serta
Shaw Flooring
South Sea Rattan
Stanley
Sunrise Furniture
Supreme Mattress
T. S. Berry
Telescope
Tradewinds
Universal Furniture
Uttermost
Wesley Allen
Wrangler Home
Wrangler Series 47

The Lions Den ★★★★

Hickory Furniture Mart - U. S. Hwy 70 SE, Level 4, Hickory, NC, 28602

Hours: Monday-Saturday 9:00-6:00
Phone: 828-431-3034
Email: interiordesign@nctv.com
Website: thelionsdeninteriors.com
Discount: 40-50% off mfr retail
Payment: VISA, MasterCard, Personal Check
Delivery: White glove delivery

The Lion's Den at the Hickory Furniture Mart is a great place to shop for unique high-end furniture at great prices! All items are "one of a find", as owner Kim Ingle says, so the selection here changes continually.

On my most recent visit, I found a good deal on a beautiful solid mahogany high boy by Theodore Alexander (pictured on the next page). This high boy retails for $16,999.00, but you can buy this one from The Lion's Den for $8,999.00. That's a savings of $8,000.00, or 47% off retail.

You may find any high-end brand during your visit, but these brands are usually represented: Theodore Alexander, Maitland-Smith, Chelsea House, Marge Carson, and Hickory White. All of the furniture here is in first-quality condition. Discounts run about 40% to 50% off retail.

The customer service here is excellent. The owners will take orders by internet or phone if you have something in particular in mind. You're also welcome to browse in person. All orders are paid in full and ship right away.

Due to the unique nature of the furniture and accessories you will find here, none of your purchases are returnable. All orders are shipped insured in case of damage in transit to your home.

Theodore Alexander high boy at The Lion's Den

Retail: $16,999.00 Discounted price: $8,999.00
Savings at The Lion's Den: $8,000.00 = 47% off retail

The Showroom

★★★★

115 East Church Street, Martinsville, VA, 24112

Hours: Monday-Saturday 10:00-6:00
Phone: 276-638-6264
Email: showroom@fm-a.com
Website: fm-a.com
Discount: 50% to 60% off mfr retail
Payment: VISA, MasterCard, American Express, Discover, Personal Check
Delivery: White glove delivery

The Showroom in Martinsville, VA is a reputable deep discounter with access to some very nice lines. They have a great reputation for service, and I find their staff very pleasant and helpful. Their discounts tend to run about 50% off retail.

Their prices are frequently lower than the deep discounters in High Point and Hickory on identical items. Before placing a special order with another discounter on any of the lines they carry, definitely call The Showroom to compare prices.

They also have a very nice line of custom occasional and dining room chairs. Customers can choose from one of 195 styles arranged around the upper walls of the showroom and have their chairs stained and upholstered any way they wish. They also have a few styles of occasional tables that can be custom stained as well. You can even send them a sample of your own furniture (a drawer or leaf) and they will stain your chairs to match.

If you've found a bargain on a lone dining room table at a factory outlet or clearance center, as I recommend, this is a good place to get special order chairs to match. Be sure to keep a leaf from the table with you so that the The Showroom can match the finish color exactly for your chairs.

If you plan to order custom chairs here, you may wish to stop by 1502 Fabrics in High Point first to pick out a fabric. They stock a huge selection of discontinued fabrics from many of the local furniture factories. They have terrific bargains. Some fabrics are as low as $1.50 a yard!

All of the furniture discounters and factory outlets owned by the Martin family have had spotless records with the BBB for many years with no complaints whatsoever. I've always been very pleased with how they've worked with my private clients and shopping tours.

If you plan to visit High Point, you may wish to take a day to drive to the Martinsville, VA area, which also has outlets for Hooker, Lane, Pulaski, and Bassett plus a clearance center for The Showroom right down the street.

Vendor carries 25 manufacturer's lines

A.A. Importing Company	Fairfield Chair	Sarreid
Action by Lane	Hekman	Stanley
APA Marketing	Hooker	Sumter Cabinet
Bassett	Kessler	Taylor King
Bassett Baby/Juvenile	Kincaid	Ultimate Accents
Bentley Churchill	King Hickory	Woodmark Furniture
Butler Specialty	Lane	Wynwood
Councill	LeatherTrend	
Drexel Heritage	Passport	

Theodore Alexander Factory Outlet ★★★★

416 S. Elm St., High Point, NC, 27260

Hours: Monday-Friday 10:00-5:00,
Saturday 10:00-3:00
Phone: 336-884-0285
Email: None
Website: theodorealexander.com
Discount: 60%-75% off mfr retail
Payment: VISA, MasterCard, American
Express, Personal Check
Delivery: Third party shipping only

The Theodore Alexander factory outlet in High Point has moved again, for the third time in three years. It is now on Elm St., right behind the former Atrium Furniture Mall. This is the only remaining Theodore Alexander factory outlet, now that the outlets in Burlington and Hickory have closed.

They have some very beautiful and unique pieces here, at very good prices. I found a great bargain on a beautiful burl veneer cherry cabinet during my most recent visit (pictured on the next page). This cabinet retails for $8,400.00, but you could buy this one at the outlet for $2,400.00. That's a savings of $6,000.00, or 71% off retail.

Theodore Alexander is known for very interesting occasional furniture and chairs. They have some very striking accessories as well. Theodore Alexander makes the Althorp Living History line of reproduction furniture from original pieces at the childhood home of Princess Diana, so you might find a few of those pieces in stock when you visit as well. The occasional pieces here are the most fun, and the best way to make the biggest design splash for your money.

The stock here consists of first quality floor samples, discontinued styles, overruns, customer returns, and photography samples. The vast majority of pieces here are in first quality condition. The discounts range from 50%-75% off retail, with most items marked about 60% off.

Please note that this outlet is very low frills. As noted on the sign that cheerily greets shoppers right inside the door, they do not provide packing materials or arrange shipping. They will give you a card with the number of a local shipper, and leave you to arrange the rest yourself.

The prices are incredible, but before buying anything here be sure to call the local shipper first to see how much you might have to pay to have your furniture properly packed and shipped to your home.

Cabinet from Theodore Alexander

Retail: $8,400.00 Discounted price: $2,400.00
Savings at the Theodore Alexander Factory Outlet: $6,000.00 = 71% off retail

---

Vendor carries 2 manufacturer's lines

Althorp Living History   Theodore Alexander

Transit Damage Freight (Kannapolis) ★★★★

Cannon Village - 251 West Ave., Kannapolis, NC, 28081

Hours: Monday-Friday 9:00-5:00, Saturday 10:00-6:00, Sunday1:00-6:00
Phone: 704-938-9010
Email: info@cannonvillage.com
Website: transitdamagefreight.webs.com
Discount: 40%-50% off mfr retail
Payment: VISA, MasterCard, Discover, Personal Check
Delivery: Customers must make own arrangements to take furniture home

Transit Damage is much more than just a typical damaged-freight liquidation center. Yes, they do have a small amount of furniture damaged in shipment or separated from it's original paperwork, but most of their stock at this particular location is made up of floor samples, discontinued styles, and seconds. They can also special order some lines.

On a recent visit, I found a great deal on a complete "Dillon" leather living room set by Bradington Young (pictured on the next page). This set has top grain leather, down cushions, and 8 way hand tied springs. You could get the matching sofa, loveseat, and chair for $3,825.95. That's a steal! The furniture had no flaws I could find. That's approximately 50% off retail for comparable sets from Bradington Young.

The brands available here vary widely and will change every visit. They accept furniture from factories, retailers, and truck lines all over the U. S., so there is no set list of lines carried.

This source isn't necessarily worth a separate trip, but if you're in the Kannapolis area anyway, you may wish to stop in. The prices are good, but not as good as in a typical factory-owned factory outlet. Most of the furniture here is priced at about 40%-50% off retail. The bargains here vary widely from not-so-great to fantastic.

Bradington Young "Dillon" sofa at Transit Damage Freight

Estimated retail for 3 piece set: $7,650.00 Discounted price: $3,825.95
Savings at Transit Damage Freight: $3,824.05 = 50% off retail

Transit Damage Freight (Lexington) ★★★★★

1604 S. Main St., Lexington, NC, 27292

Hours: Monday-Thursday 9:00-5:30, Friday 9:00-7:00, Saturday 9:00-5:30
Phone: 336-248-2646
Email: None
Website: transitdamagefreight.webs.com
Discount: 40%-80% off mfr retail
Payment: VISA, MasterCard, Discover, Personal Check
Delivery: Third party shipping

Transit Damage is much more than just a typical damaged-freight liquidation center. Yes, they do have a small amount of furniture damaged in shipment or separated from it's original paperwork, but most of their stock at this particular location is made up of floor samples, discontinued styles, and seconds from nearby factories like Linwood, Lexington, and others.

The outlet is huge, with three enormous metal warehouses filled with all types of furniture. Discounts vary widely, with most pieces in new, first quality condition at about 40%-50% off retail.

The real steals are the pieces with miniscule damage, but big discounts. I found one such bargain on a recent visit: a Bob Mackie Classics bedroom set by American Drew, including the sleigh bed, nightstand, armoire, dresser, and mirror (pictured on the next page). This set retails for $16,340.00, but you could buy this one set at Transit Damage Freight for $3,900.00! That's a savings of $12,440.00, or 76% off retail!

And what was wrong with it to justify such a huge discount? A little ding on the side of the bed that can be easily fixed with a touchup pen in about five minutes. That's well worth saving $12,000.00 to many shoppers!

This is a great source! They have a huge selection with furniture in new condition at 40% to 50% off retail, and furniture with very minor damage at up to 80% off retail. If you don't mind doing minor restoration work, you can get some amazing deals here!

Bob Mackie bedroom set at Transit Damage Freight

Retail: $16,340.00 Discounted price: $3,900.00
Savings at Transit Damage Freight: $12,440.00 = 76% off retail

Small flaw on bed easily touched up

Tyson Furniture Company

109 Broadway, Black Mountain, NC, 28711

Hours: Monday-Saturday 9:00-5:30
Phone: 828-669-5000
Email: sales@tysonfurniture.com
Website: tysonfurniture.com
Discount: 40%-60% off mfr retail
Payment: VISA, MasterCard, Discover, Personal Check
Delivery: White glove delivery

Tyson's Furniture Company in Black Mountain, NC, just east of Asheville, is huge. It occupies about a dozen interconnected buildings covering more than a city block in downtown Black Mountain. You could spend all day browsing here!

On my most recent visit, I found a great deal on a 3 piece leather "Bedford" group from Lexington (pictured on the next page). This 3 piece set retails for $8,391.00, but you could buy this set at Tyson Furniture for only $2,999.00. That's a savings of $5,392.00, or 64% off retail! The set was in new condition.

Most of the furniture here is new first-quality, priced at about 50%-65% off retail. If you shop here in person, be sure to ask for their extra 10% discount for cash purchases made in-person at the store.

Please note that Tyson Furniture will charge sales tax on your shipment if your home state requires it. While you will find other deep discounters who won't insist you pay taxes owed to your home state, honestly, those other stores are not doing you any favors. When you don't pay at the time of purchase, many states will send you a bill weeks or months later demanding the sales taxes owed plus penalties. Florida and California are particularly known for high penalties on unpaid sales taxes. Tyson Furniture is handling sales taxes the right way, which really is in the best interests of the customer.

Tyson Furniture has an A+ rating with the BBB, and a spotless reputation. They've been owned and operated by the Tyson family since they opened in 1946. Their customer service is very good. I've never heard a single reader complaint about them. I highly recommend this source!

Lexington leather living room set at Tyson Furniture

Retail: $8,391.00 Discounted price: $2,999.00
Savings at Tyson Furniture: $5,392.00 = 64% off retail

Vendor carries 186 manufacturer's lines

A-America	Bramble Company	Cochrane Furniture
A. A. Laun	Braxton Culler	Company C
A. J. Floyd	Brooks	Conrad Grebel
Abner Henry	Broughton Hall	Cox Manufacturing Co
Alfresco Home	Brown Jordan	Craftique
American Drew	Brown Street	Cresent
American Woodcrafters	Broyhill	CTH Sherrill Occasional
Appalachian Rustic	Bucks County	Davis Cabinets
Armstrong Vinyl	Butler Specialty	Decorative Crafts
Artistica Metal Designs	Cape Craftsmen	Designmaster
Aspen Furniture	Capel Rugs	Distinction Leather
Bassett	Carolina Furniture Works	Dixie
Bassett Mirror	Casabique	Drexel Heritage
Benicia Foundry	Century Furniture	Durham Furniture
Bermex International	Charleston Forge	Eastern Accents
Bernhardt	Chatham Furniture	Ekornes
Better Homes	Chromcraft	Elite Leather
Bigelow Commercial	Classic Flame	Emerson et Cie
Bob Timberlake	Classics by Casabique	Englander Bedding
Boling Chair	Clayton Marcus	Fairfield Chair
Bradington Young	CMI - Colonial Mills	Fashion Bed Group

Fauld

Feizy Rug

Ferguson Copeland

FFDM

Ficks Reed

Flat Rock Furniture

Fremarc Designs

Furniture Classics Ltd.

Gat Creek

Gonzalez & Associates

Guy Chaddock

Hammary

Hanamint

Hancock & Moore

Heather Brooke

Hekman

Henkel Harris

Henredon

Hickory Chair

Hickory White

Highland House

Hillsdale Barstools

Hinkle Chair

Hooker

Howard Miller

Human Touch

Hunt Country Furniture

Huntington House

Interactive Health

Jessica Charles

Johnston Casuals

Justin Camlin

Kaiser Kuhn Lighting

Karastan

Kessler

Kincaid

King Hickory

Kingsley-Bate

KNF Designs

Koch Originals

La Barge

La-Z-Boy

Lafuma

Lane

Laneventure

Lea Industries

Legacy Classic

Leisters Furniture

Lexington

Linwood

Lloyd/Flanders

Lorts

Lyndon

MacKenzie Dow

Magnussen Home

Maitland-Smith

Master Design

Meadowcraft

Midi

Mohawk

Motioncraft

Nautica Home

New River Artisans

Nichols & Stone

Old Hickory Furniture

Old Hickory Tannery

Palatial Leather

Palecek

Palmer Home

Parker Southern

Paula Deen Home

Pennsylvania House

Peters-Revington

Powell

Pulaski

Quality Cushion Factory

Randall-Allan

Regency House

Riverside Furniture

Royal Patina

Royal Teak

Rug Market

Sam Moore

Sealy

Seven Seas Seating

Shadow Mountain

Shaw Flooring

Simmons

Sligh

Somerton Furniture

South Sea Rattan

Southern Living

Sovereign

Stakmore

Stanford

Stanley

Statesville Chair

Statton

Style Upholstery

Summer Classics

Superior Furniture

Sutton

Taylor Vance

Telescope

Temple

Tempur-pedic

Tennessee Enterprises

That Place

Theodore Alexander

Tom Seely Furniture

Tommy Bahama

Tradewinds by LaneVenture

Trans-Ocean Import Co

Treasure Garden

Tropitone

Troutman Chair

Trump Home

Two Day Designs

United Furniture

Universal Furniture

University Loft Company

Uwharrie Chair

Valco

Vanguard Factory Outlet

★★★★★

Hickory Furniture Mart - U. S. Hwy 70 SE, Level 4, Hickory, NC, 28602

Hours: Monday-Saturday 9:00-6:00
Phone: 828-322-3471
Email: info@goodshomefurnishings.com
Website: goodshomefurnishings.com
Discount: 50%-75% off mfr retail
Payment: VISA, MasterCard, Discover, Personal Check
Delivery: White glove delivery

The Vanguard Furniture Factory Outlet is managed by Good's Home Furnishings. You'll find a very good selection of high end upholstery here, along with some case goods.

Discounts range from 60%-75% off retail. Most of the pieces here are discontinued items or floor samples in first quality condition. It's rare to find a piece with any damage in this showroom.

On my most recent visit, I found a fantastic deal on a beautiful "Bloomsbury" queen sized upholstered bed in perfect condition (pictured on the next page). This bed retails for $5,019.00, but you could buy this one sample bed for $1,999.00. That's a savings of $3,020.00 or 60% off retail!

The customer service here is excellent. I highly recommend this source!

"Bloomsbury" bed at the Vanguard Furniture Factory Outlet

Retail: $5,019.00 Discounted price: $1,999.00
Savings at the Vanguard Furniture Factory Outlet: $3,020.00 = 60% off retail

Wellington's Fine Leather Furniture ★★★★

233 Selma Circle, PO Box 1817, Boone, NC, 28607

Hours: Monday-Friday 9:30-5:30
Phone: 828-295-0491 / 800-262-1049
Email: hampwell@fineleatherfurniture.com
Website: fineleatherfurniture.com
Discount: 30%-40% off mfr retail
Payment: VISA, MasterCard, American Express, Discover, Personal Check
Delivery: Curbside delivery is free. White glove delivery is $149.00 per order

Wellington's Fine Leather Furniture is a great source of American made leather. They sell furniture by Distinction Leather, Leathercraft, Bradington Young, Pallister, Palatial Furniture, and McKinley Leather.

They are a very reputable company with an excellent BBB rating. Special order prices run about 40% off retail. Wellington's offers a limited selection of in-stock items at about 60%-70% off retail at their website.

They have a great deal on shipping if you are located in the 48 continental U. S. states: free curbside delivery on orders over $999.00. You can upgrade to full white glove inside delivery for an extra $149.00 per order.

All of the lines they carry are high quality with hardwood frames and eight-way hand tied springs. All of the furniture from this source can be ordered with spring-core cushions, but this is not standard on some models. Consumers should ask specifically about spring-core cushions, which will last much longer than foam-core cushions. This is a great source!

Vendor carries 8 manufacturer's lines

Bradington Young	Flexsteel	Palatial
Coja Leatherline	Leathercraft	Palliser
Distinction Leather	McKinley Leather	

Brand Index

B (con't)

Bramble Company	75, 153, 182
Brass Craft	109
Braxton Culler	23, 45, 66, 75, 109, 117, 153, 161, 163, 170, 182
Breezesta	66
Brent Jacobs	75
Bridge Bay	17
Bridgewood Dining	17
Brimar	75
British Traditions	153
Brooks	137, 139, 147, 149, 182
Brookwood	75
Broughton Hall	75, 123, 124, 125, 147, 149, 182
Brown Jordan	13, 75, 153, 182
Brown Street	15, 153, 182
Broyhill	34, 45, 75, 104, 109, 117, 123, 137, 139, 141, 147, 149, 182
Brunschwig & Fils	13
Brunswick	17
Brushstrokes	75
Bryson Bedroom	17
Bucks County	182
Builtright Chair	161
Bulova	75
Burlington	17
Burton James	98
Bush Furniture	75
Butler Electric	75
Butler Specialty	45, 75, 85, 117, 124, 125, 145, 153, 170, 174, 182

C

C. R. Currin	13
C. R. Laine Upholstery	75, 104, 109, 153
Caffco International	75
Cal-Bear	75
Cal-Style	50, 75
Calcot Ltd	75
California House	75
California Kids Bedding	75
Calligaris	58, 68, 157
Caluco	58
Cambridge Carpets	13
Cambridge Chair	137, 139, 161
Cambridge Lamps	109
Cambridge Mills	104
Camelot Carpet Mills	13
Camerich	58
Camilla House Imports	13
Canadel	104, 117, 153
Canal Dover	17, 75, 137, 139, 170
Candella Lighting	75
Canterbury	17

C (con't)

Canvas Company	75
Cape Craftsmen	15, 75, 109, 153, 182
Capel Rugs	66, 117, 161, 182
Capris Furniture	66, 75, 109, 161
Caracole	75, 104
Carey Moore Designs	75
Carlton McLendon	170
Carolina Furniture Works	182
Carolina Mattress	141
Carolina Mirror	35, 75, 109, 141, 161, 170
Carolina Tables	107, 153
Carolina's Choice	15
Carpet Creation	75
Carrington Court	163
Carter Furniture	17, 75, 153
Carver's Guild	35, 87, 89, 91
Casa Fiora	42, 75
Casa Novalia	75
Casabique	182
Casamania Furniture	68
Casana	75
Casey Collection	75
Casprini Furniture	68
Cassady	15
Cast Classics	15, 75
Cast Craft	75
Castagnetti Furniture	68
Castelle	66, 75
Castilian Imports	163
Casual Creations	43
Casual Lamps	109
Catnapper	52, 54., 56, 137, 139
Cattelan Italia Furniture	68
Cebu Furniture	109, 153
Central Oriental	75
Century Furniture	20, 21., 30, 31, 66, 75, 87, 89, 91, 93, 104, 115, 145, 153, 161, 182
Century Rugs	50
CFI Manufacturing	75
Chandler Collection	75
Chapman Lamps	75
Charles Alan	75
Charleston Forge	15, 66, 93, 98, 104, 153, 182
Chateau	17
Chatham County	50
Chatham Crossing	75, 153
Chatham Furniture	182
Chelsea Frank Group	75
Chelsea House	66, 75, 153
Cherry Pond	15
Chicago Textiles	75
Child Craft	75

G (con't)

Green Frog Art	75
Green Gables Furniture	17
Greene Brothers	60, 109
Greenhouse Design	75
Greenwich	17
Gregson	35
Griffin Creek	75
Guardsman	31, 75
Guildcraft of California	123
Guildmaster	75, 104, 109, 153
Gunlocke	75
Gus*	58
Guy Chaddock	75, 85, 182

H

H Studio	64, 124, 125
H. Bridges	75
H. K. H. Intl	75
H. Potter	75
Habersham	31, 35, 75, 87, 89, 91, 163
Halcyon	75
Hallmart Collectibles	75
Hamilton Collections	75
Hammary	45, 75, 93, 104, 109, 117, 137, 139, 147, 149, 161, 170, 182
Hammerton	161
Hampton Bedroom	17
Hampton Hall	137
Hanamint	87, 89, 91, 93, 182
Hancock & Moore	31, 35, 42, 75, 87, 89, 91, 93, 104, 153, 182
Harco Loor	75
Harden	31, 42, 66, 75, 87, 89, 91, 95, 104, 137
Hardin Lodge	17
Harris Marcus	60, 75
Harrison Import & Export	75
Hart Associates	75
Havaseat	75
HBF	75
Heather Brooke	141, 153, 182
Hedge Row Outdoors	75
Heirloom	30, 75
Hekman	42, 45, 66, 75, 87, 89, 91, 93, 104, 109, 117, 139, 145, 174, 182
Hellenic Rugs	75, 137, 139
Hemsley	75
Hen-Feathers	75
Henkel Harris	31, 35, 85, 87, 89, 91, 153, 182
Henredon	20, 21., 31, 66, 75, 85, 87, 89, 91, 93, 96, 182

H (con't)

Henry Link	35, 66, 75, 87, 89, 91, 109, 135, 180.
Heritage	17
Heritage House	15
Hickory at Home	104
Hickory Chair	35, 45, 87, 89, 91, 93, 104, 153, 182
Hickory Classics	45
Hickory Heritage	42, 75, 98, 137, 139
Hickory Hill	50, 139
Hickory Mark	50
Hickory Springs	75, 137, 139, 161
Hickory White	20, 21., 42, 75, 93, 107, 182
High Point Furniture	35, 75, 109, 153
High Smith Furniture	75
Highland House	30, 66, 75, 87, 89, 91, 115, 124, 125, 182
Hillsdale Barstools	117, 137, 139, 153, 182
Hillstreet Beds	137, 139
Hinkle Chair	182
Historic Golf Prints	75
Holga	75
Holiday House Sleepers	50
Holland House	117, 137, 139, 153
Hollin Gate	102, 115
Holly Springs	137, 139
Hollywoods	75, 109
Holton Galleries	75
Home Fires	75
Home Source	87, 89, 91
Home Treasures	75
Homecrest	43, 161
Homelegance	27, 45, 52, 54., 56, 109, 117, 147, 149, 170
Hooker	20, 21., 35, 73, 75, 85, 87, 89, 91, 93, 117, 119., 121, 137, 139, 141, 145, 147, 149, 153, 170, 174, 182
Howard Elliott Collection	75
Howard Miller	35, 45, 50, 75, 87, 89, 91, 93, 109, 117, 124, 125, 137, 139, 153, 161, 182
Hubbardton Forge	75, 137, 139
Hugh Moffitt	75
Human Touch	75, 182
Humane Trophies	75
Hunt Country Furniture	153, 182
Huntington Furniture	75, 124, 125
Huntington House	75, 87, 89, 91, 182
Huppe	68, 75
Hurtado	75
Hyland Park	17

L (con't)

Lucia Cassa Textiles	75
Luke Leather	123, 137, 139, 153
Luna Bella	13, 163
Lux-Art Silks	75
Luxembourg	17
Luxy Furniture	68
Lyndon	182
Lyndon Furniture	58
Lynnwood	17
Lyon Shaw	43, 66, 75, 109

M

M. T. S. Besana-Carrara	75
MacKenzie Dow	30, 117, 153, 182
Madison Square	35
Magis Design Furniture	68
Magna Design	75
Magnussen Home	42, 45, 50, 60, 75, 93, 109, 117, 124, 125, 137, 139, 147, 149, 153, 163, 170, 182
Maharam	75
Maitland-Smith	13, 35, 66, 75, 87, 89, 91, 93, 102, 115, 117, 143, 153, 182
Majestic Mirror	75, 87, 89, 91
Mallin	75
Manchester Furniture	75
Manhatten	17
Manor Meyhaus	17
Mansour Rahmanan & Co	75
Mantua Manufacturing	75
Maple Creek	17
Marbella	17
Marcella Fine Rugs	75
Mardan Publishing	75
Marge Carson	75
Mario & Marielena	75
Mariposa	13
Mark David	75
Mark Roberts	75, 87, 89, 91
Marquis CLL	75
Marquis CSTM Contract	75
Marshall James	87, 89, 91
Martha Stewart	75, 93
Marvel	75
Mary Mayo Designs	75
Masland Carpet & Rugs	13, 75
Mason Maloof	75
Mass Imports	75
Massoud Furniture	153
Master	17
Master Design	45, 109, 124, 125, 137, 139, 170, 182
Master Woodcraft	17

M (con't)

Mastercraft	75
Masterfield	15
Masterlooms Rugs	75
Masterpiece Accessories	75
Mathews and Company	13, 75
Matrix	75
Mayer Fabrics	75
Mayline	75
McGuire	35, 153
McKay Table Pads	15, 75, 141, 153
McKinley Leather	30, 153, 187
McNeilly Champion	75, 123
Meadowcraft	35, 75, 87, 89, 91, 93, 182
Med Lift	137, 139
Memphis	17
MER Rugs	75
Mercatus	58
Metropolitan Galleries	75
Michael Thomas	35, 87, 89, 91, 153
Michael's Mission	17
Midi	182
Midj Furniture	68
Mikhail Darafeev	75, 104, 109
Milan Bedroom	17
Miles Talbott	75, 87, 89, 91, 98, 153
Millender	75
Millennium	52, 54., 56, 124, 125, 147, 149
Miller Desk	75, 161
Milling Road	93
Minoff Lamps	75
Mirador	75
Mirage	17
Miresco Rugs	137, 139
Miriam	17
Mirror Craft	75
Mission	17
Mobel	15, 45, 87, 89, 91, 109, 117, 153, 170
Mobican	58
Mod Loft	58
Modern History	153
Modern Shaker	17
Mohawk	15, 75, 87, 89, 91, 182
Momeni	75
Momentum Textiles	75
Montaage	75
Montage	75
Montecito Dining	17
Montrose	17
Moore and Giles	75
Moosehead	153
Morgan Hill	13, 153

M (con't)

Morganton Chair	50
Motioncraft	75, 85, 87, 89, 91, 93, 153, 182
Movi	75
MTS	75
Muniz Acrylic Furniture	64
Murphy Wall Bed	17
Murray Feiss Lighting	13, 75, 87, 89, 91
MWB Designs	75
Mystic Valley Traders	75, 87, 89, 91

N

N. C. Souther	75
Nan Wood Hall Fine Art	75
Naos	75
Napa Home and Garden	13, 75
Napsax by Artisan's Guild	75
Natale Furniture Industries	75
National Mt. Airy	35
Natural Light	75
Nature's Gallery	75
Natures Rest Marketing	75
Natuzzi	58, 75, 157
Nautica By Lexington	180.
Nautica Home	75, 182
NDI	75, 87, 89, 91
NE Kids	75
Nelson Garfield	75
Neutral Posture	75
New Albany	17
New Century Picture	75
New England Dining	17
New Haven	17
New River Artisans	66, 75, 117, 182
New River Bedroom	17
Newport Cabinet	153
Nichols & Stone	109, 182
Nirvana Swing Co.	75
Noah's Mission Bedroom	17
Noonoo Rug Company	75
North Bay Collections	75
North Hampton Dining	17
Northern Fine Arts	75
Norwalk Furniture	153
Nuance Fine Furniture	75
Nuevo	58
Null Furniture	15, 60, 75, 109

O

O'Asian	35
O. D. E. Fine Art	75
O. L. F.	75
O. W. Lee	75
Oak Designs	153
Oggetti	58

O (con't)

Ohio Table Pad	15, 50, 109, 137, 139, 153, 170
Oklahoma Importing	75
Old Biscayne Designs	13, 104, 161
Old English Mission	17
Old Hickory Furniture	75, 161, 182
Old Hickory Tannery	104, 153, 182
Old Java	75
Old World Stone & Iron	75
OLF Lamps	75
Olympia	75, 87, 89, 91
Omnia Leather	45, 133
Oopsy Daisy	75
Opus Designs	75, 153
Orbit	75
Orderest Bedding	15
Orient Express Furniture	104, 147, 149
Oriental Lacquer	109
Oriental Weavers	75, 117, 157
Origlia Furniture	68
Orleans	75
Osborne & Little	13, 75
Oscar de la Renta	75
Our House Designs	153
Outdoor Classics	43
Outer Limits	58
Overnight Mattresses	98
Overnight Sofas	117, 170
Ozark Cedar	161

P

P & P Chair	15, 75, 153
Pacific Coast Lighting	75
Padma's Plantation	31, 66, 75
Paladin	104, 117
Palatial	187
Palatial Leather	87, 89, 91, 153, 182
Palecek	75, 109, 117, 153, 182
Palliser	42, 45, 75, 93, 117, 124, 125, 170, 187
Palmer Home	180., 182
Palmyra	75
PAMA	75, 153
Paper White	75
Paragon Picture	75, 87, 89, 91, 109
Park Avenue Lamps	75
Park Place	15, 109
Parker House	109, 137, 139
Parker Southern	50, 75, 104, 182
Passport	145, 161, 174
Pastel	60, 75, 153
Pastel Furniture	58
Pastiche	75
Paul Robert	87, 89, 91

CPSIA information can be obtained
at www.ICGtesting.com
Printed in the USA
LVHW051051281021
701787LV00009B/157